Surrounded
by
God

Surrounded

by

God

A Journey Through Trauma, Grief & Forgiveness

Karen Freres

ISBN: 978-0-578-59990-8

The events and conversations in this book have been set down to the best of the author's ability from her own memories. Some names and details have been changed to protect the privacy of individuals.

Unless otherwise stated, all Scripture quotations taken from the HOLY BIBLE. Scripture quotations marked (NIV) are taken from THE HOLY BIBLE, NEW INTERNATIONAL VERSION®, NIV® Copyright © 1973, 1978, 1984, 2011 by Biblica, Inc.® Used by permission. All rights reserved worldwide. Scripture quotations marked (AMPC) are taken from the Amplified® Bible (AMPC), Copyright © 1954, 1958, 1962, 1964, 1965, 1987 by The Lockman Foundation. Used by permission. www.Lockman.org Scripture quotations marked (AMP) are taken from Amplified® Bible (AMP), Copyright © 2015 by The Lockman Foundation. Used by permission. www.Lockman.org. Scripture quotations marked (KJV) are taken from the KING JAMES VERSION (KJV): KING JAMES VERSION, public domain. Scripture quotations marked (NKJV) are taken from the New King James Version®. Copyright © 1982 by Thomas Nelson. Used by permission. All rights reserved. Scripture quotations marked (MSG) are taken from THE MESSAGE, copyright © 1993, 2002, 2018 by Eugene H. Peterson. Used by permission of NavPress. All rights reserved. Represented by Tyndale House Publishers, Inc. Scripture quotations marked (TPT) are taken from The Passion Translation®. Copyright © 2017, 2018 by Passion & Fire Ministries, Inc. Used by permission. All rights reserved. ThePassionTranslation.com. Scripture quotations marked (NLT) are taken from the Holy Bible, New Living Translation, copyright © 1996, 2004, 2015 by Tyndale House Foundation. Used by permission of Tyndale House Publishers, Inc., Carol Stream, Illinois 60188. All rights reserved.

Front and Back Cover Images & Design by Matthew Freres.
Book Interior Formatting & Design by Matthew Freres
Website: www.matthewfreres.com

Edited by John T. Freres III
Creative Editing by Matthew Freres

Printed in United States of America.
First Printing Edition 2019.
E-mail: surroundedbygod@gmail.com
Facebook: fb.me/surroundedbygodbook

To my best friend John,

I love you and miss you! Most of all, I forgive you. I know there is so much more to this story, and when I get home to Heaven, you can tell me all about it.

TABLE OF CONTENTS

Preface

As I write this, I am asking myself, "How many people really read the preface?" I'm going to guess there are two types: the people who love to read and soak in every inch of the book, and then those others who just want to get to the meat of the book and view the preface section as unnecessary fluff. Full disclosure, I fall in the latter. For those of you who do read this preface, I would love to give you a quick look at my thoughts behind the book.

To be completely honest, I had many reservations about writing this book at all. If it were totally up to me, I don't think I would have followed through with it. I am definitely introverted and am quite happy to not share my personal life with lots of other people. So, you can imagine that sharing my story of trauma and pain is way outside of my comfort zone. However, one of the biggest lessons I've learned through my trials is that life is not all about me. God revealed to me that if I want my pain to have a greater purpose, I need to share it with others who might find hope and healing in my story. For that reason, and that reason alone, I was willing to step out of my comfort zone.

I have felt God nudging me to write this book for the past few months. I thought about the idea and played around with several ways of trying to get it written, but the problem is that I am not a writer by any stretch of the imagination. I have never even been a big reader either, and I would definitely have to say that, for me, writing is a weakness instead of a strength. The funny thing about God is that He will often ask us to do things that we are not good at, and this was no exception. The reason He does this is so that He gets all the glory. The only reason this book exists is because God chose to work supernaturally through me. It is truly miraculous the way this was written.

As I said before, I was playing around with several ideas about writing this book. Well, I think God could see that I wasn't making much progress but was pleased that I was willing to try. What happened next was nothing less than a miracle. One day, out of nowhere, there was an overwhelming amount of information in my head, and I couldn't think about anything else. I had been trying to verbally record it all on my phone, in hopes of someone else actually writing it, but God just kept telling me to go to the computer and write! So, write I did. I still don't exactly know how it happened, but in less than two weeks the book was written. I cannot take credit for it. All I did was show up and partner with God. He did what I could never do on my own.

To be honest, there were times when the writing was very difficult because it required me to revisit so much of the pain and deep emotions from all I have endured. So, during much of this process, I would have Bethel Music videos playing while I'd write. It was as if God was holding my hand during the entire writing process. There were many times I would have to stop and cry, as I would remember the moments of deep pain, but because the music was playing, it was ministering to my soul, bringing healing to those areas that still need it. It was the fuel to keep me writing. It was a reminder that God is always with me. To you, the reader, about to go on this journey with me, I hope that in the midst of this raw, honest story you would see the beauty of all God has done for me. This is the story of how God surrounded me in all of my pain and how I finally forgave Him.

Thank You

"The King will reply, 'Truly I tell you, whatever you did for one of the least of these brothers and sisters of mine you did for me."
Matthew 25:40 (NIV)

As much as I would love to be able to thank every person individually that helped our family during the most difficult time of our life, it's just not possible. The list is seemingly endless, as so many people stepped up and performed countless acts of kindness for our family. So, at the risk of leaving someone out, due to my limited memory, I didn't want to take the chance of excluding anyone. If you were one of those people who helped our family in any way, big or small, please know that it all mattered and helped get us to safe harbors. The verse above is confirmation that although you may not have received worldly recognition, your Heavenly Father sees and knows your acts of kindness, and you have laid treasures in Heaven. Let me take this brief moment to say thank you on behalf of our family. Know that you are all a part of our story. I have prayed many times that God would bless each of you.

There is, however, one person that I feel I must recognize by name. My dear friend Tonya played such a monumental role in our story. Not only does Tonya's heart run deep with passion and empathy for others, but her willingness to help is off the charts! She is extraordinarily gifted when it comes to planning and executing just about anything! Even in the wake of tragedy, she never blinked an eye in helping and putting a plan to action. Without her loving heart and willingness, in combination with her areas of giftedness, this story would have looked much different. I often pray that God would bless her for all of her selfless acts of kindness, not only for our family but for all the countless others that she has cared for. I can hear our Heavenly Father saying to Tonya **"Well done, good and faithful servant!"** (from Matt 25:21 NIV). So, Tonya, please know how much you are loved and appreciated by our family and, most importantly, by God.

A Blessing

For each and every one of you reading this book, I bless you! My prayer is that no matter where you're at on your journey with God, that you will be blessed in some way and gain some nuggets of truth that will positively impact your life.

If you don't have a relationship with God, I still pray that you will be blessed and that this book will help you see God in a new light, as He loves everyone and is always waiting with open arms.

If you have been walking with God for a very long time, I pray that God will bless you with a deeper understanding of who He is for you.

For those of you in a season of deep pain, I bless you to give yourself permission to be real with God, no matter what you have been through. He will meet you right where you are.

No matter where you're at on your journey, just remember that life is just that: a journey. I bless you to never get stuck along the way. Even if you go backward for a while, just keep moving, and eventually, you will get going in the right direction.

Most of all, I bless you to receive all of what God has for you in your lifetime and to discover your Kingdom purpose. It's even more beautiful than you know.

Chapter 1

My Fallen Knight

It all started as a child, playing with barbie dolls up the street at my friend's house. We had the entire basement to ourselves and were allowed to set up Barbie houses, leaving them in place for weeks on end. We would all set up our houses, decorating them with the perfect furniture (that was often homemade), and filling them with all of the things that we dreamed of having one day. We would set up Christmas trees with presents wrapped under the tree (in miniature Barbie sizes, of course) in hopes of playing out the best Christmas scene ever. We went all out!

I can remember running up the hill to my friend's house every day after school to continue each scenario from the day before. We would just keep building on the stories of the lives we dreamed of, getting more and more detailed about what went where, and who got what accessories or pieces of furniture. I would be lying if I said that we never fought over some of the most precious items and outfits for our Barbie homes, as we wanted to have the best of everything. Although no one ever "won the game", it was always kind of unspoken that the one with the nicest house and family would be the envy of us all.

The most important part of our Barbie game though was choosing which Ken doll you would have for the husband/dad in your family. This was critical. Choosing your husband and deciding what he did for a living was in fact the thing that would really set the tone for how well you did the rest of the game. So, as you can imagine, there were a few fights over this one. Funny how real life starts to play out at such a young age.

At a deeper level, this is where I started dreaming about my future husband that I would have in real life one day. I actually believe that due to playing this Barbie game, I had determined at a pretty young age that I was setting my expectations high! I wanted a Knight in shining armor! Someone who could be that Ken doll in the Barbie game. Someone who was perfect, who would take care of me and our kids better than anyone else could. Someone who would sweep me off my feet and keep me there. Someone who would always be there for his family and always take care of us. A best friend for life. This is what I had my heart set on.

Eventually, I was no longer a child playing a game of Barbie, and I became an adult whose dream came true! I met my best friend. My Knight in shining armor; uniform and all! His name was John and he was a helicopter pilot in the Marines who walked with such honor. I instantly knew this was my husband. We immediately became best friends, and after a short courtship, we were married. He was everything I had dreamed of. Life soon filled up fast with four beautiful children and all that goes with raising a family. Our life was full but good. Sadly, as most of us know, life doesn't always stay good. There are always curve balls and trials. We were no exception to this. For years, we encountered trial after trial. Some were very painful, causing us to dig deep and fight for our beautiful marriage. However, we were determined to get through anything, as we truly were best friends.

With each trial, we grew stronger in our conviction to get through whatever life threw our way. Even though we had to deal with some very difficult issues, it always seemed okay because we had each other and had learned to rely on God to do what we could not do. In fact, all the trials and difficult seasons had developed a strong faith in us. However, this faith soon became tested as we entered our most difficult season yet. Things became harder than ever before, but having built up a faith in God over the past twenty years, I never stopped believing that my husband and I, with God, could get through anything. I had faith that God was always going to be there for us as He always was before.

However, everything was about to change in a single phone call...

On January 11, 2010, I was not prepared for what I was about to encounter. On that cold January day, I was driving with my oldest son, on the way to pick up my youngest daughter from basketball practice. The phone rang and we were hoping it would be my husband, as we had been waiting for him to call to plan my son's trip back to college. Since I was driving, my son answered for me. He put the call on speakerphone, and I heard an unfamiliar voice start speaking to me. This voice asked if she could speak to Karen Freres, and I replied, "This is her." She asked me if I was driving, which I thought was a bit odd, and I reluctantly said yes. She asked me if I could pull the car over to the side of the road, and I immediately felt strange. She waited until I could assure her that I was in fact pulled over and parked on the side of the road. She asked if anyone was with me, and I replied, "My oldest son". Then, she calmly stated that she was the coroner and that she had some bad news. She proceeded to explain that my husband had been brought into the morgue and that it appeared that he had killed himself. My son and I just looked at each other with no words, in total disbelief. She asked me several more questions, of which I have no memory. My mind was too busy trying to process the horrible, life-changing words she had just spoken to me.

It is difficult to truly explain what I was experiencing at that moment. No matter how I write this out, I won't fully be able to do it justice. So, I will do my best to paint a picture of what those moments were like.

It's amazing how one side of the mind can have so many things racing it through it all at once, while the other side can feel completely empty. It was as if all of life went blank, while at the exact same time, I was keenly aware that my life had just changed forever. I immediately knew that I just lost my best friend, the father to my children, and my provision. All of the things I had hoped and believed for our family, that I had invested my life into, were all gone in a single moment. I could feel something in me trying to rise up to resist this information that my mind was not wanting to process. It was like I was trapped in a soundproof box screaming "Nooooooo!", but no sounds were coming out of my mouth. Then a flood of thoughts entered my mind:

"How do I tell my other children?" "This was not part of my life's plan!" I just kept thinking, *"No God, I don't want to tell the children that their dad is gone! This is not ok!" "What the hell just happened?" "This must be some kind of mistake!" "This is a mistake, right?" "You would never allow this, right, God?" "John would never leave the family he loved so much." "No! This is not real!"* **"God, I thought we had a deal?!"** *"I thought that as long as I made you the God of my life and built my life around you that you would always help me when I needed it!" "Is this your way of helping me?!" "I have been crying out to you over the past year for help and this is how you are going to help me?!" "I have spent the past twenty years learning how to rely on You for help, and although You have allowed many trials thus far, never anything like this. You've always helped us get through them with the hope that things would get better!" "I trusted You!" "This was not part of the deal!" "This is a whole new level! I'm not prepared for this!" "There was no training for this!" "This is so final! There is no hope in this!" "How in the world am I going to get through this!?"*

My husband and I were a team. We had spent years learning how to be good partners in life. I always believed that with God, we could get through anything, but I never believed that God would allow this! My Knight in shining armor had now fallen and perished. I knew full well that God could have stopped this, but now I was forced to ask the question, "Why didn't He?"

Chapter 2

A Prelude to Receive

Before I continue, I want to back up and give you a glimpse into the year prior to this phone call to help you better understand everything we were going through. This prior year would prove to be a very painful one. I would have to watch my husband deal with an issue that was clearly breaking him down. What was even more painful was that I was unable to know exactly what that issue was. To this day, I still do not fully understand everything that my husband was dealing with prior to his death.

Before the start of that year, things had become very difficult for us financially. My husband had always done well in the business world, but things were slowly starting to unravel, and it was unknown to me as to why this was happening. The best way to describe it is like that of a puzzle: I had many of the pieces, but I was missing some of the most critical ones, making it impossible for me to fully put the picture together of what exactly was going on behind the scenes with him. While the tension around our finances had grown exponentially, nothing could have prepared me for what was about to happen at the start of that year.

Almost exactly a year before the phone call about my husband's death, we lost our home on the coldest day of the year. It was so cold that school had been canceled and my kids had to stay home. This is one of my most painful memories and is incredibly difficult to have to revisit. So, in order to avoid having to get into every painful detail, I will describe it like this: in a matter of hours, we were without a home, and all of our things were being piled outside in our very snowy driveway. I told my kids to grab their most valuable belongings and pile them in the van. With nowhere to go, this would prove to be one of the most difficult days of my life. If it had not been for the dozens of people who showed up to our house at a moment's notice, packed up all of our things, found a moving truck, and a storage facility to hold it all, we would have lost most of our possessions.

I remember driving around in my van, dealing with the pure shock of what had just happened, and trying to figure out where we would go. My phone rang. It was my friend telling me she just learned about a family from the kid's school who had a rental house not too far away from where we had been living, and we could rent it from them. They would also allow us to bring our pets. The house happened to be vacant due to renters who had moved out early, so we were able to move in immediately. It was a complete miracle! God's swiftness met us on one of our most traumatic days.

Still, it was such a traumatic event that it is even difficult writing this short summary. I had many nightmares after this event. I would wake up in the middle of the night and feel like someone was coming into our house to kick us out, which caused so much emotional stress. To be honest, it took me years to work through the pain from that day.

One day, years afterward, while praying to God to help me work through the emotional stress I was having from remembering the pain of that day, He gently asked me to see it differently. I felt it was impossible to see it any differently than the horrible day that it was, but I felt Him saying, **"I want you to see what I see. I want you to see all the wonderful people who ran to your aid in that horrible moment. I want you to see that it was I who activated all of those people to do what you could not and that I always go before you and make preparations, even in the difficulties of life. From now on, whenever you recall that day, I want you to only focus on that! Not the bad, but on how I rescued you because that is who I am. I will always be there for you, no matter what."** That moment with God has helped tremendously every time I start to recall that day. When I find myself starting to feel the pain of that memory, I am quickly reminded of that moment with God and choose to see it through His eyes, finding a greater sense of peace as I do.

Learning to see these memories through His eyes has been crucial in my journey.

The months following the loss of our home would prove to be some of the most challenging we had ever faced. However, I had not lost faith, as I saw how graciously God had taken care of us by instantly providing help and a house for us to stay in. Even though things were really difficult, I never stopped believing that God was making a way forward. Every day was a faith journey. I was being stretched way beyond anything I had ever experienced before. This season began to teach me the true meaning of living by faith and not by sight.

Truthfully, that entire year would prove to be difficult, yet somehow, we managed to get by. Eventually, we moved into another rental house, and I was hopeful things would finally start to improve. My husband and I were on our knees daily, sometimes hourly, praying and trusting that God had better for us. I was aware, however, that there were things going on with my husband that were way bigger than he could handle. Things were clearly out of his control. Not having the other critical puzzle pieces, I was unable to make total sense of what was going on. We even sought help from a trusted pastor and counselor that we had worked with in a previous season, but unfortunately, it wasn't helping whatever was going on behind the scenes. All I knew was that the enemy was involved in trying to take my husband down, and my only hope was to go to God and trust that He would take authority over the evil that was happening in my husband's life.

"Be well balanced and always alert, because your enemy, the devil, roams around incessantly, like a roaring lion looking for its prey to devour" 1 Peter 5:8 (TPT)

This was such a difficult place to be. I wanted so badly to help in some way. I would literally pray hourly just to get through most days. I had no other choice but to trust God to do what I could not do. Even in those difficult days, God would show me that He was, in fact, still with me, and on most days, that was all I had to cling to.

On one particular day during that year, we came to a point where we had run out of money and food. My husband explained that he would be getting paid soon, but that we had nothing for the moment. I found myself at a new low, wondering how we went from living such a nice life not that long ago to now having no food. Not knowing what to do, I found myself at our church's food pantry. I had never been to a food pantry before. It was very humbling, to say the least. Unfortunately, the line there was long and moving really slow. I waited in line for as long as I could, but it was late, and I needed to get back home to help the kids get ready for their next day of school. So, I left before I could get any food. I felt so bewildered and thought, *"God if I could just have some bread, then I could make the kids and I some toast."* I drove home in silence, asking God over and over again for some bread.

For the first time in my life, I now knew what it was like to truly feel hungry. It quickly brought to mind all the millions of people on this planet who live like that every day. Feeling exhausted, and not knowing what to do, I just drove home and tried to ignore the fact that we had no food. I had only been back home for a few minutes, and my son Matthew called from his friend's house, telling me that my friend Tonya (his friend's mother) had given him bags of groceries to bring home to our family! I was speechless. I had not told anyone that we had no food or money (probably out of embarrassment). My friend knew that we were in a very difficult financial situation, but she had no way of knowing that I had just come back from the food pantry. After many tears shed from the kindness of my friend's generosity, I had to ask what made her go buy us bags of groceries? She said that she felt God tell her to do so. If any of you ever doubt that God speaks, let me just say that He does!

In previous years, when our family had been doing well financially, I loved getting to bless others who were in need. I especially enjoyed giving gifts and money, often in secret. One of our favorite things to do was to pile in our van and go do secret drop-offs at the homes of people in need. Being able to help these people had been such a source of joy, but now God had turned the tables. I was now in a season of being the one in need.

Let me be honest: this was not easy for me. I loved being the giver, but I did not like being the receiver. It was extremely uncomfortable. I had never really thought of what it would feel like to be the receiver, I mean, what it "really" felt like to be the receiver. I assumed it was wonderful to receive gifts and money you weren't expecting, but I hadn't really thought much beyond that. I was so grateful that my friend was very gracious in not making a big production out of giving us the bags of food. She simply served us in as private a way as possible. I realized at that moment, not only is it important to serve others but to do so in a way that allows the receiver as much dignity as possible, as they are most likely dealing with several humbling issues all at once.

As humbling as it was, what I find so beautiful about this story is that in my place of desperation and hunger, I asked God for just a bit of bread. Instead, He brought me bags full of all kinds of groceries. Even at my lowest place, His favor and love for me was not limited.

God's timing is impeccable, as my friend's gift of groceries, moving me from giver to receiver, came just about a month before the phone call of my husband's death. Little did I know how necessary that transformation was, as I was about to enter a life-changing season in the wake of my husband's death that would require me to receive more than I ever had before.

Chapter 3

The End is Now the Beginning

As soon as I received the phone call about John's death, life became a big blur very fast. Family and close friends started arriving at our home as soon as the first calls were made. This was clearly uncharted territory for everyone. Few knew what to even say, except to join with us in our crying and give us hugs. There were so many blank stares of disbelief and so many questions I did not have the answers for. People kept showing up to drop off food, money, and more hugs. They also brought more questions, and I continued to have no answers. My close friend, Tonya, (an angel, really) quickly took over directing the flow of chaos, as she could see that I was in no shape to handle all that was going on around me.

Everyone just kept telling me to breathe. I can vividly remember times in those first few days after the phone call when all I could focus on was taking a breath in and then letting it out. For days, people would just remind me of this simple action. As strange as it sounds, it's like my body would forget, and as soon as someone would remind me, I would think, *"Yes, I need to breathe."* So many thoughts were running through my head at times that I would just forget to breathe. Then other times I wouldn't be able to think at all. Sometimes it hurt so bad physically from all the trauma that I would just want to fall asleep, but I couldn't. Honestly, it felt like some kind of torture. I remember feeling utterly sick to my stomach much of the time. The truth is, if not for my four precious kids, I am not sure I would have been able to make it through this trauma. So, when I would feel my absolute worst, the mother-bear deep inside of me would rise up to say, *"No! I am going to fight through this!"* I just kept thinking, *"My kids deserve someone to fight for them. I will fight until my death for them. I have no idea how on earth we are going to make it through this, but I am going to fight with everything I have for them!"* Then, I would remember to breathe again.

I would continually go back to the thought that it was all a big mistake. There was at least some hope in this thinking. I would hear my phone ringing in the other room and think, *"Maybe that's John, and he's going to tell us it's all ok."* I hadn't yet seen John's body, which allowed me to entertain this thinking. But then, slowly, my spirit would slip back into reality: the reality of how my entire life had just changed in a phone call, and that life would never be the same again. I was forced to come to grips with the fact that all that I was hoping for had just been ripped out of my hands. I had never planned or played out this kind of scenario in my childhood barbie game! This process would then repeat itself every time I started to hope that there might be some kind of miracle.

One of the moments that stand out from those first few days would be the moment my husband's best friend, Tony, showed up at the house. It was the closest thing to having John walking through the door. Tony and John were similar in so many ways, and when you were around one of them, you would be reminded of the other. Our families are close, and it was almost like I could sense John's spirit when Tony arrived. He brought a deep sense of peace in such a dark moment. Tony is also a pastor, so it felt even more safe to process and be comforted by him. I remember all of us sitting on the couches in our family room, just staring at each other in disbelief without having a whole lot of words. We were all just sitting there, trying to wrap our minds around what had just happened and why. I remember my little dog, Gizmo, jumped up on the couch and immediately curled up next to Tony, resting his head on his lap. This might not seem significant, but if you knew Gizmo, it was! Gizmo would never immediately just sit next to a non-family member, let alone put his head on their lap. Gizmo treated Tony almost as if he was John. We all sat there for a moment, just observing the spiritual significance of this action. Even if we couldn't explain it, we all knew it was somehow supernatural.

Adding to our growing support network, some of my oldest, most dear friends from out of state, who I hadn't seen in years, dropped everything and flew in for the week to help us. I will never forget the feeling I had when they walked in the door. It was like a warm blanket that brought such a strong sense of God's peace and comfort! God was clearly showing that He was putting an army of warrior friends around me to help carry the load and protect me. They would prove to be an incredible help in the time they were with me. Working nonstop, they did what I could not, helping make decisions I was unable to make.

Due to the very difficult financial season we had been going through, we quickly realized that we had our work cut out for us, as I had no money. We were in a rental house with no money to pay the rent and had just discovered that rent was behind several months. As a result, the homeowner would not allow us to stay. We would have to pack and move out in one week, which would be the day after we buried John. Not only were we planning the funeral, which felt exhausting in itself, we were also having to get an entire house packed and ready to move out the day after the funeral! We didn't even know where we were moving to! At the time, I had four kids, four dogs, a cat, two birds, and several other rodents (I think). We had a mini zoo! I had no idea how in the world were we going to find a place to live that would accommodate all of us, and without money to pay rent!

All of this was going to require a miracle from God. Actually, several miracles! As the reality of all this settled in, I found myself slipping away. I had no power over my life. I was at the total mercy of God. I had known many difficulties in my life thus far, and God had always intervened at the exact moment I needed Him to, but this, this was a whole new level of needing God. I found myself asking more questions: *"Can I really trust Him now? After all, He just allowed this unbelievable event to happen, altering my life forever. Can I trust Him to help me now? Maybe something in my relationship with God has changed? Maybe He is no longer interested in helping me?"* Although the terrifying reality around me was pressing me to agree with these fearful thoughts, I knew I couldn't continue with that line of thinking. The reality they were inviting me into was simply too grim. I knew I was going to have to dig deep and choose to believe that after years of seeing Him come through for me, He was somehow going to do so again. Even though I was so baffled as to how, and why, He allowed this to happen, I would still choose to put my hope in Him and put my disbelief aside for a later time. The need to survive was simply too strong, and I knew I couldn't survive without Him.

I also quickly realized I did not have the mental or physical capacity to handle all that would be required over the coming days and weeks. So, I relinquished my power of attorney to my most trusted friend, Tonya. She was the only person I knew who was equipped to pull off everything that was needed for planning a funeral and an entire move in one week. She really was an angel in human form! She had already done so much for me over the years, and now she was stepping up in the midst of her own busy life to take on her most difficult task to date, all on my behalf.

Something you hope you never have to do is go to the morgue to identify your loved one...

It is as horrible as you can imagine. At least, it was for me. When it came time to go to the morgue and identify John's body, my oldest son, J.T., decided to go with. We knew it was going to be a hard experience, so Tonya and her husband, Randy, insisted on taking us.

Upon reaching the coroner's office, reality started to set in. I started feeling sick to my stomach. My knees buckled, and I became so weak and dizzy that Tonya, Randy, and my son had to help hold me up as we entered the front lobby.

We were first taken into a very cold and uneventful room with a long table and some chairs. We waited there until they were ready to take us back to where the body was kept. My husband's belongings were lying on the table for me to identify and retrieve. The reality set in deeper. Feeling sicker and sicker, I wondered how I would make it through the next five minutes, let alone view my husband's body. I could see in J.T., Tonya and Randy's eyes that they were feeling the same way but were trying to stay strong on my behalf. I remember feeling so bad that they had to do this with me, but I knew I could not have done it without them there to hold me up. They were like my angels in that dark place.

After what seemed like an eternity, but was probably only 10 minutes or so, the coroner finally came back in the room to take us to see my husband's body. We slowly walked down a hall that led to the room that held John. It's hard to describe the reality of what I experienced in that room, but I will say this: If I did not believe in the reality of Heaven, knowing beyond a shadow of a doubt that my husband's spirit was already there, and that we were just looking at his empty earthy shell, I would have surely hit the floor. The reality began to sink in: **my best friend of 22 years would no longer walk this earth with our kids and me.** It was more than I could handle.

While viewing his body, my mind was trying desperately to convince myself that I could see him breathing! I'm not sure if this happens often to people in this situation, but for me, it was so real! Maybe it was my mind's way of trying to deny the truth that was before me. I just kept looking and was so sure I saw him move!

Then, J.T., with tears in his eyes, began to read from his Bible over my husband. One of the verses he read was John 3:16: "For God so loved the world that He gave His one and only Son, **that whoever believes in Him shall not perish but have eternal life.**" (NRSV) I was so touched and amazed that he had the mental ability to have planned to bring his Bible and speak God's word over his dad! I could barely breathe, and he was selflessly blessing his dad with the only truth he could cling to: the promises of God, of eternity in Heaven. It's moments like this where true character in a person really shines bright, and my son exhibited character beyond his years! Tonya and Randy were standing there with us as we all processed this horrible moment together. I know it was awful for them as well, and yet they also showed incredible character by helping us through this most difficult task with nothing but love and care!

Just to prove how real God is, as I sit here working on this chapter right now, I am listening to Bethel music on YouTube, as it helps comfort me while recounting the difficult memories required to write this. Right at the exact moment when I started writing the sentence about John's spirit being in Heaven, the song "Ain't No Grave" by Bethel Music came on! If you have never heard the song before, look it up, and you will understand how powerful this moment was for me. This also illustrates how God always finds a way to let you know He is there with you, even in the pain.

Later that day, after being at the morgue, we only had a little bit of time to go look at some rental homes my friend had found. Because I was not in a position to make any financial decisions, my amazing, loving mother said she would take care of the rent until we figured things out. Thanks to her, we were now able to go look for a place to live.

So, we all piled into cars to look at some rental homes. It all felt so surreal, like I was living someone else's life, or playing a character in a movie. I was just at the morgue identifying my husband's body, and now I was trying to find somewhere to live!? It didn't seem real, and yet, here I was. As we were all sitting around the table at one of the rental homes, getting ready to sign a lease with the homeowner, I suddenly felt something inside of me say, *"No!"* I was a bit shocked and got up from the table to go into another room. My friends followed me to see what was going on and all I could say was, "No, this is not the house we are supposed to live in." I knew that God was speaking to me and guiding me. So, we politely said we were sorry, that I couldn't sign the lease, and then we left.

Then someone reminded me that another family friend from our church had offered us to stay in their vacant lake house for the next few months, and they wouldn't even charge us rent! We had already looked at their lake house earlier but dismissed it, thinking it would be way too small for all of us and all our pets. But God spoke clearly and asked me to go back and see it with a fresh set of eyes.

When we went back to see the lake house again, I knew immediately that this was where God wanted us to be. God knew I wasn't thinking clearly, and so He was helping me to make the better choice. Rent-free was definitely the better choice in our situation. Even though it was going to be a smaller space for all of us, and most of our things would have to go in storage, God knew a smaller space would be best for now. It also helped that it was owned by an amazing family from our friend group. I was so overwhelmed that they would be so gracious to let us stay there! Pets and all! Free of charge! This was one of many ways God showed me His goodness and faithfulness in the darkest hour of my life. He had sent me more angels in human form!

Chapter 4

God at the Grave

Sitting in a funeral home, planning a funeral you do not want to plan, is a horrible feeling no matter how you slice it. It just continually reminds you of the reality you are facing. What's more, in the midst of all your grief, you are forced to make many decisions and they are all expensive. I was so overwhelmed at this point that I just didn't really care about the money anymore. I figured that God would somehow work that part out.

Honestly, it was a struggle just to stay focused through this whole process. While much of it is a big blur to me, I do have some vivid memories of this time. One of them is all of us standing in a circle, holding hands and praying, while at the funeral home. I just remember saying to God, "Where else would we go, but you God?" I felt completely lost and overwhelmed. All I could do was cry out to God to help us and trust Him to do what I felt so unequipped to do. I knew He was the only hope to get my children and I through this horrible nightmare.

"God's angel sets up a circle of protection around us while we pray" Psalm 34:7(MSG)

Another thing I vividly remember was the man who took care of us at the funeral home. Somehow, he was so incredibly comforting. Another angel in human form! He made it as painless for us as he possibly could! He seemed to understand at a deep level what I was going through. I knew nothing about him but could feel his genuine care and concern for our family and situation. He stayed by our side throughout the entire event. There was just something supernatural about his presence! I can't fully explain it. He was literally by my side, comforting me in a way I don't have words for. I often wonder if he really was an angel. I know that might not make sense to many reading this, but for me it does. Whoever he may have been, I thank God for him.

"God sends angels with special orders to protect you wherever you go, defending you from all harm." Psalm 91:11(TPT)

When I look back at this phase, I realize how many people were stepping up left and right for us, doing things that we just couldn't do ourselves. In the whirlwind of everything, I was unable to acknowledge and properly thank every one of them for all of the ways they served us. I remember people shopping and buying clothes for my kids to wear to the funeral, putting deposits down for the cemetery, providing and paying for a limo for our family on the day of the funeral, bringing food and more food, donating time and money, and helping us to prepare to move. One family even opened a bank account with money in it so we would have something to live on. Another church family, who owned a moving company, donated their time and trucks to move us the day after the funeral. There are so many more people that I can't even recall. I have prayed so many times that God blesses each and every person who served our family in any way. I know we would have never made it through those days without every one of them! Again, God was revealing himself through the care of others.

There was a part of me that was very challenged with this whole process, as I am normally very self-sufficient and do not like to ask for help at all. However, I was so overwhelmed mentally and emotionally, that I was unable to do what needed to be done, and I truly needed all the help I could receive. I felt like a part of me was dying inside as I continually released more and more control. I remember our house just being filled with people over that week leading up to the funeral, sorting through everything and getting things packed for the move. It was so overwhelming to me, yet I was in the most vulnerable place, desperately needing this newfound support.

However, there were some things that I only I could do. For instance, since John had been in the Marine Corps, he was entitled to a military funeral.

If there was one thing I knew that John would have wanted, it would have been to have a military service, as being a Marine was in every cell of his being. It was the last and only gift I felt like I could truly give him this side of Heaven. In order to give him the military service, we had to produce a document called a DD256. I had no idea where this document would be, as I had never seen or needed it before, and I had no idea where to look. This was going to take a miracle to find. Without it, there would be no military burial, as the funeral home needed this document to request a formal military burial at the funeral. There were many phone calls made to see if there would be a way around this, but with no success. We prayed, "Lord, please help us find this document!" We found a box of photos and paperwork that John's mother had given us before her passing a few years prior. We must have gone through that messy box at least twenty or thirty times, hoping that the DD256 would be in there, but we had no luck.

So, we started putting our focus on other things, feeling horrible that we might not be able to give John the proper funeral that he so deserved. While I was focused on the next task at hand, I heard my youngest son, Luke, say, "Is this what you're looking for?" Amazingly, it was in fact the document that we so desperately needed. Although we had moved on to other things, Luke had patiently stayed focused on that messy box, going through it methodically, piece by piece. Then, he came across a photo in a frame. For some reason, he decided to take the photo out of the frame, and when he did, he found the document behind the photo!

In my opinion, this was a miracle! This was something that was so important to us, and in the midst of all of the pain and disbelief, God was showing us again that He was, in fact, right there with us. Not only was it important to us to see that John was buried with honor, but it was to God as well. John had served our country with honor for almost a decade, and we wanted to see honor given to him as he was laid to rest. It would have been horrible to bury him without the American flag on his casket and the Marines standing so proudly at his graveside, playing "Taps", as we said goodbye for the last time.

The day of the funeral finally arrived. We had planned it to the best of our ability in the midst of all we were dealing with. It felt surreal, going back and forth between preparing to move and preparing for the funeral. I don't think I even knew what I was wearing to the funeral until the night before. I found the one black outfit that hadn't been packed, that was comfortable, and that's what I wore. I felt so unprepared, as there was no time to get myself looking somewhat presentable. I had very little sleep in the few days leading up to it, and I had cried my eyes out countless times.

I felt overwhelmed just trying to function, let alone meet and greet a large number of people at the church. If it was not for our family and close friends surrounding all of us, planning every little detail and making so many decisions for us, I would not have been able to get through that day. At some level, I was aware that my family and close friends were concerned as to whether I would even make it through the service. I was also feeling very concerned, as I physically didn't feel like I could go on much longer. Thankfully, God will often give us supernatural strength in the moments we need it most. I can remember feeling so weak physically, and God just kept supernaturally sustaining me one moment at a time. While the trauma has blocked out much of my memory from that day, I have never forgotten how He carried me so perfectly in my weakness.

"My grace is sufficient for you, for my power is made perfect in weakness" 2 Corinthians 9 (NIV)

Watching each of our children put notes and special items in John's casket was definitely one of the most emotional things for me to witness. All these years later, it is still very difficult for me to even think about it for too long. It still is so painful! I also remember feeling very overwhelmed at the amount of people who showed up on that cold January day to show their respect for John. There were so many people I had not seen in years; some I had never seen or met at all. As I greeted each person, I genuinely tried to stay in the moment with each of them, but then I would quickly see the long line of people and think, *"How in the world am I going to make it through this?"*

Interestingly, a theme began to build as I spoke to each person. As I met more and more people that I didn't know or had only met briefly through my husband's work, I was hearing a similar theme from many of them. They would all tell me that John had impacted their life in a powerful way. I began to hear over and over again about how John had helped them when no one else would. They would say things like "He gave me a job when everyone else turned me down" or, "He got me connected with the right people when no one else would help me" or, "He really encouraged me and helped me figure out a way forward when there didn't seem to be one." Over and over, I was hearing these kinds of things about John. These were all stories I had never heard before.

God was revealing to me in this most difficult moment that John's life, although ended much too soon, had impacted so many other lives in such a positive way! I remember one man telling me that if it wasn't for John helping him, he didn't know what he would have done, as he had been in a desperate place and John's help got him back on track. Unfortunately, we ran out of time and I wasn't able to greet everyone who had come. It was a tight schedule that day and I remember feeling bad for the people I didn't get to speak with. They may have had more wonderful things to say about John, which would have been therapy for my heart. In such a horrible time, I felt that those stories provided, at some level, redemption of the life he lived. Amidst all the pain and trauma, I saw that the mark John left on this earth was much bigger and more beautiful than I had known.

As we moved to the next section of the funeral, I suddenly became so aware of each of our four kids. It was as if God was allowing me to feel what it must be like for each of them losing their dad. It honestly was all too much. It took everything I had to try and keep my composure, as the internal battle was so strong and real. I wanted to huddle up my four kids and run out of the church as a way to protect them from what was staring them in the face. I had felt a similar feeling many times throughout the week prior, but for some reason, it hit me so powerfully in that moment. It was all-consuming and difficult to focus on anything else.

As Tony began the service and started sharing some wonderful memories of John, I immediately felt a sense of peace come over me. Again, Tony's presence reminded me so much of John that it was extremely comforting. He then began to share some absolutely hysterical stories about him and John. Listening to the church break out in laughter during these stories was so life-giving. The truth is, John was an extremely funny guy, and he and Tony shared an amazing connection, especially with their humor. Their similarities were undeniable and during some of the moments when Tony spoke, I could actually feel John's presence. Even to this day, when our two families get together, I feel the peaceful presence of John because of the bond that they shared.

To understand this next miracle, I need to back up to a few days prior to the funeral. My oldest son, J.T., had been crying out to God, asking Him to show us that He was real, and that John was indeed in Heaven. With all the intense pain he was feeling, he especially needed God to confirm these things to his heart. As he was crying out to God, he had a vision: *three deer in the cemetery where we would lay John to rest.* He shared this vision with me and a few others. For our family, deer hold a lot of meaning. Years earlier, deer had become a way that God would show Himself to us. Whenever we were struggling with something, right at the exact moment we would be praying and asking for His help, deer would often show up.

So, on the day of the funeral, we were all in the limousine our friends had graciously provided, allowing us to all ride together. It was so relieving to just sit together and not have to worry about driving. As we were riding from the church to the cemetery, J.T. put his head back and fell asleep. A short time later, as we pulled into the entrance of the cemetery, my son Matthew yelled "Deer!" As J.T. lifted his head, he immediately saw three deer running together in the cemetery! We all looked with amazement, as we knew of J.T.'s vision! Our hearts knew God was saying, **"I am real. I am here with you. John is with me in Heaven, and everything is going to be okay."** In my opinion, it was another miracle. Even close friends around us were moved by the way God spoke through these deer. Looking back, I realize that God knew our hearts needed that sign in order to get through the coming days.

We had chosen to bury John in the military section of the cemetery, and as we pulled up to it, the realization hit me: *"This is it. I am saying one final goodbye to my best friend."* As I sat there, staring at John's casket with the American Flag still draped over it, I remember feeling overcome with a deep sadness that I had never felt before. The kind of sadness that knows no words, only the silent groans of the heart. The only other thing that sticks out in my mind is hearing the sound of "Taps" playing in the distance, and then watching the Marines meticulously folding the flag from John's casket. Once the flag was folded, in perfect ceremonial fashion, one of the Marines presented the flag to me, and I remember him looking me directly in the eyes and saying, "On behalf of the President of the United States of America, the United States Marine Corps, and a grateful nation, please accept this flag as a symbol of our appreciation for your husbands faithful service." That moment remains engraved in my mind, as I knew how proud John would have been to receive those words. So, I received them for him. I clung to that flag as it was all I had left of John. It was then that my heart was truly broken, as my best friend, my Knight in shining armor, was now gone.

Typically, there would be some kind of event or meal following a funeral. However, in our case, time did not allow for this, nor were we in any mental capacity to process with others about all that had just occurred. We had to go home and prepare for the enormous task of moving the very next day. We were so exhausted emotionally and physically, running on such little sleep, that all we could do was to go home and try to nap before preparing for the move. It just felt so surreal, burying my husband in one moment and packing up and moving our whole family in the next! Nevertheless, the task was facing us. There was no choice but to just kept moving through it, like wading through mud up to our chest.

I remember the day of the move being one big blur. My mind had hit a threshold and I felt like a zombie. The only thing I clearly remember were my friends walking me through the house and asking me questions. With the lake house being much smaller than the house we were moving out of, we had to put most of our things in storage, only taking with us what was most important. Room after room, they would walk me through and ask me to point out what was to be put in storage and what would go to the new house.

I remember seeing so many people packing and cleaning for us as we walked through the house. It felt so overwhelming because I was unable to verbalize my gratitude to them in the moment. Under normal circumstances, I would have been doing all of that work myself, as I loved a good project. However, at this moment, I felt completely inadequate, and was deeply moved by all of the people (some I didn't even know) showing up to selflessly serve our family. My mind was jumping between a deep sense of gratitude for all of the people helping us and then trying to focus on all of the decisions needing to be made. I remember struggling hard just to think, let alone make decisions about what we might need or what should go into storage. I had no idea what lied ahead, what our life would look like, or how long we would be living in this new temporary house. It often felt like it was taking everything just to survive, and I had no idea how I was supposed to make all the decisions before me, given the state of trauma I was in. I remember frequently asking friends, "Can you just decide this for me?"

Besides feeling overwhelmed with gratitude for all of the people helping at the house, I don't really remember much else from that day. I don't even really remember the first night sleeping at the lake house. Looking back though, without all of those amazing people in my life who selflessly served our family, things would have been so bleak. What was really happening was that God was showing Himself to our family through all of these people, holding us faithfully through all of this newfound pain. He was surrounding us in the midst of tragedy with countless people acting as the hands and feet of Jesus.

Chapter 5

The Frozen Lake

God was purposeful in putting us in our friend's lake house. Even though it was a tight fit with the five of us, our four dogs, a cat, and a few birds, we made it work. The view of the frozen lake each day seemed to be very fitting for the season we were in. Although a cold, dark season, it was somehow peaceful in a strange way. This at least felt better than all of the chaos that had just been swirling around us.

I remember the first time the sun came shining through the windows of the lake house, and I thought to myself, *"I wonder if my life will ever shine again?"* I knew in my spirit that there was a long, hard battle ahead. It was one I wasn't even sure I could win, especially with a God who had just allowed so much trauma. I now wondered what other horribly traumatic things He would possibly allow. I knew deep down I was going to have to tackle the big question with God: *"Why would You allow this?"* However, there was still so much to deal with each day, that I knew I did not have the time or energy this battle would require. It would have to wait for a later season.

Much of this phase has been lost in memory. I do remember being completely tired most of the time. We all slept as much as we could, as it helped us physically and mentally cope with all the trauma we now had to somehow sort through and make sense of. Sleeping allowed us a break from trying to process the overwhelming pain. But then you'd wake up, and there it was, staring you in the face, reminding you that your life is different now. It's like someone plucked you out of your old life and dropped you in some new life in a foreign land. You just want to go home, but you can't. That life is gone now. It's never coming back! These intense feelings are reserved only for those who have walked through deep loss and trauma. Unless you've walked through it, you could not possibly understand the deep pain in this season, nor would you want to. Somehow, our family was chosen to be included in this special group; a group none of us ever wanted to join.

I found myself printing out Bible verses and hanging them all over the walls of my bedroom. I needed to have something to look at, to try and hope for, as life seemed so bleak. I needed to cling to the only truth I had known, even though I had so many questions. These verses would prove to be a foundation, a place to go when I felt that I had nothing.

Those first few months were filled with many things that I did not feel like doing, but had no choice, as they needed to be dealt with. There was so much paperwork! Sending death certificates to umpteen places, phone calls and more phone calls, applying for Social Security, and the list goes on. This phase was very difficult for me. It was such a vulnerable time, having to have all these people and entities in my personal business! As an introverted person, this was a horrible feeling. It was difficult for me because I needed everyone's help, and yet, I have always been wired up to do things on my own, requiring much less interaction with others. I also tend to be more of an independent and self-sufficient person. This deeply independent quality of mine and my pressing need for so much help seemed to contradict one another, and I was caught in between. In a season where I had so much to process internally and would have preferred so much more time alone, I was forced to interact with others for many of those days.

While I wanted more time to be alone, I never wanted any of my friends or family to think that I wasn't grateful for all they were doing for me. I loved spending time with them, and I would have enjoyed my time with them even more under better circumstances. I was often in an internal battle of wanting to be fully present, but also feeling the need to go be alone and process my life. Looking back, I am grateful for my friends and family who were wise enough during this phase to just keep showing up, even if I wasn't very present. They knew that it would take some time for me to handle things on my own. So, they watched over me, gently guiding me and caring for me in every way they possibly could.

I did not have the strength at this point to fight, at least not very hard. This was difficult territory, even for the caretakers around me. I realize now that everyone was doing the best they could through this uncharted territory. They all knew that at some point I would have to get back on my feet, but none of us knew how or when that was going to happen. Everyone knew it was going to take miracles from God! Yet, they were in it for the long haul. So, they just kept loving on my kids and I the best they knew how. I'll say it again, they were angels in human form!

One of the most comforting things I remember from this time was food. In our state of shellshock, our close friends would bring us food and groceries. Night after night, week after week, they would faithfully take care of all of our food needs. I can remember feeling God's love over every meal. It's amazing how good food can taste when you don't have to prepare it. Even if I wasn't hungry, which was much of the time, once I would smell the food that was dropped off, I would instantly get hungry. I can remember sitting with the kids each night, having these meals together, and feeling so much gratitude for the people who had taken the time to prepare them for us. It created a special time for us each day where we didn't have to do anything but show up at the dinner table and eat together. We would literally enjoy every piece of food that was sent over. There was something so heavenly about each meal. I can't fully explain it, but in such a difficult time, it was a comfort that we truly looked forward to each day.

"For when you saw me hungry, you fed me. When you found me thirsty, you gave me something to drink. When I had no place to stay you invited me in," Matthew 25:35(TPT)

The truth is, none of us had the energy to cook. So, if others hadn't been so gracious in bringing the meals, those evenings together would have not been the same. It was God slowly creating a new normal. Even if it was small, it was something. Each day was filled with so much uncertainty, but at least we all knew there was going to be a dinner together and it was going to be delicious.

The best way I can describe to you what I experienced in the weeks and months following John's death is through the image of me walking on a tightrope. I went through this phase on and off for quite some time. I would feel my spirit being pulled towards Heaven. I know that may sound weird to some, but now my very best friend was there, and part of me longed to go there to be with him. But of course, at the very same time, my four precious children were here, and I would never leave them. I would fight to my death for them. Still, there was at some level, a desire to see my husband. So the image of a tightrope would appear in my mind, and I would often find myself on the tightrope, trying to balance, and wanting to be in both places at the same time. Logically, I knew that was impossible, but I knew my spirit was actually capable of experiencing the realm of Heaven while staying somewhat present here on Earth. So I would often find myself balancing on that tightrope, and actually finding a sense of peace there. The more time I would spend doing this, the more I would let go of earthly things. This process was aligning me with a heavenly perspective and helping men let go of what didn't really matter. This was so important in helping me get a clearer image of what was most important in life.

In a way I cannot fully explain, there was a part of me that was relieved for my husband; knowing that he was out of his pain and suffering, knowing that he no longer had to deal with the evil that was facing him in this world. He was now home, in complete joy and peace with his ABBA Father. My flesh was feeling the anguish of not having him here on Earth, but my spirit, at some level, felt so grateful for the place of peace he was in now.

I remember the first night after John's death. My two oldest sons dragged their mattresses into my room so they could sleep on the floor. J.T. brought his laptop in and played several YouTube videos before we fell asleep. They were all clips of the British Bible scholar N.T. Wright speaking about Heaven. In one video he spoke about Luke 23:43. Before Jesus died on the cross, He told the thief on the cross next to him that "today you will be with me in paradise." (NIV) According to N.T. Wright: "Paradise is an ancient Persian word which means 'a garden - a lovely, beautiful garden.' And it's a word which was in common use at the time to mean a place of rest and refreshment and delight." I remember laying there in the dark and crying. Although I was so heartbroken and devastated, I found deep comfort in the fact that John was now safe and at peace in the garden of Heaven. It was like God was shining a light down on me in the midst of the darkness and allowing me a small glimpse of the wonderful place John was now in.

John and I would often high five each other when one of us was taking a break and the other one was taking charge of the house and the kids. Almost like a changing of the guards, we would high five each other and say, "I got this, so go and enjoy." I couldn't help but see the image in my mind of us high fiving for one last time, and me saying to John, "I got this, so go and enjoy."

Several weeks after settling into what would be the new normal for a little while, a very special friend of mine, Kelly, gently invited me to go to a Beth Moore Bible study at her church. Now, to be honest, I was still in total survival mode, dealing with so many things, uncertain of what my life would look like in the weeks and months ahead. Not to mention, I was also absolutely tired most of the time. It would have been totally understandable for me to politely decline her very sweet offer, which was my initial response. However, for some strange reason which I cannot explain, I actually accepted her invitation.

So each Monday night, I would go with her to this Bible study. It was a perfect setup for me, as it was just a group of women watching a video of Beth Moore's teaching on a big screen in the dark church sanctuary. There was little need to interact with others, which was something I was in no shape to do. I would sit with her and a few of her friends who all knew what I had just been through and expected nothing from me. It was a safe place where I didn't have to do or say anything. It felt nice to be somewhere where there were no expectations of me. I could just sit and rest, surrounded by faith-filled women.

Some of the women stayed afterward for discussion time, but Kelly was wise enough to know that was not what I needed and never even suggested that I stay. She did, however, know that there would be prayer time after every teaching. In the front of the sanctuary would be some very sweet women available for anyone in need of prayer. I remember the first night we were there, and Kelly asked me if I would like to go up front to receive some prayer? Even though I was in a strange place with God, so unsure of our new relationship, I still knew at a deeper level that He was my only hope in surviving all this. Although I was feeling very vulnerable, I went up front anyway.

I do not remember much of the teaching from those weeks, but oh, how I remember the ladies who prayed over me! The feeling that I would experience as they would pray; the tears that were shed. Clearly, this was a divine plan to get me into the presence of God. I would just receive the love of others who could be strong and fierce in the spirit, who would stand in the gap for me, as I had no power to fight for myself. These were not just average women saying safe, halfhearted prayers. They were spiritually mature women who had the gift of prayer and were anointed to pray in a way that would move mountains! They were prayer warriors who understood the true power of prayer. They prayed in teams over me, week after week. Some prayed out loud, some in their spiritual language of tongues, each with great love and care, expecting nothing in return. They prayed because it brought them great joy to serve in this way.

Each week would roll around, and on some weeks I would feel so tired that I would consider not going, but my kids would immediately say "No! Mom, you need to go to Bible study because you are better when you come home." So each week I would muster up the energy to go, and each week I would go for prayer. It didn't matter to those amazing women that I would go up to the front every time and ask them to pray over me again. There was no shame. It was a safe place for me to release so much pain.

Other than the women who were praying, there were usually very words spoken at all. Often, I would cry through the entire prayer time. I always felt the presence of God there. So much so, that I would often not want to leave. I quickly developed a special bond with one of the ladies who prayed over me most weeks. Even though we never spoke much to each other, my spirit knew that she was someone who walked closely with God, and it felt so safe to be in her presence.

Kelly had the spiritual wisdom to know there was little she could really say to help or comfort me in this early stage, but she knew her weapons well: Prayer! She was a spiritual warrior that God had so graciously put into my life. I can honestly say that she was a lifeline for me. Although I could not see them, she saw such amazing things ahead in my journey and would slowly speak life over me amidst all the darkness.

As Kelly and others would pray over me, something was happening. There was a spiritual battle going on over the life of my family, and each time they would pray, advancement was being made in the heavenly realm for our good. Somehow my spirit knew this, and it became the fuel to keep me moving through these difficult days. This was the very baby stage of healing. It was just the start, but it was powerful. Even as I sit here recalling those nights of prayer, of how God ministered to me in those moments, I am taken over with peace. There really is no substitute for the presence of God.

"And the peace of God, which transcends all understanding, will guard your hearts and your minds in Christ Jesus."

Philippians 4:7(NIV)

Chapter 6

Hide and Heal

Shortly before his death, my husband had started working for a new company and had been given a small life insurance policy through them. Because his death was a suicide, and because he had only been with the company a short amount of time, many around me doubted I would receive any of the money from the policy, let alone the full amount. In most life insurance policies, benefits are not paid out for suicides. My head knew this logically, but the more that those around me would say things like "You probably won't get the money", the more something inside of me would reject those comments. I knew they were just trying to be realistic and help me not get my hopes up too much, but something deep down was saying *"No! I need that money! God knows I need that money!"* A Bible verse that had been hanging in our homes for years, which read "with God all things are possible" (Matthew 19:26 NIV), just kept going through my mind. It kept repeating over and over again in my head. Even though I was hearing what others were saying, and knew it logically made sense that we probably wouldn't receive the money, I would just keep thinking *"No! With God all things are possible."*

Even though I had all of these unresolved issues with God, there was still a part of me that was refusing to believe that He wouldn't come through for us now. It really felt like it was all on the line for us. We needed that money. Even though it was a small life insurance policy, it would be just enough to get us into an adequate home and let us get our feet back on the ground. Without it, things looked really bleak. So I just kept waiting, week after week, for an answer, believing God would come through for us. Finally, the phone call came, and I was told they had approved the money and they would be sending a check. It was as if someone had just lifted a thousand pounds off of my shoulders! I knew this wasn't going to fix all of the problems that I was facing, but it would at least allow me to breathe for a while, and man, did I need to breathe.

The house hunting soon began. While we were so grateful for the lake house, it was now time to find a new home to call our own. We looked almost every day, trying to find something we could afford and still allow us the room we needed, while also staying in the school district we needed for my daughter. Normally, I love house hunting. Having grown up as a daughter of a builder, I'd love to see the potential in a house. However, this process proved to be a difficult one, as we were on a timeline and had to stay within a tight budget. Day after day, we would check the listings, hoping and waiting for the perfect home to pop up.

One day, amidst all the endless searching, I finally noticed a diamond in the rough. It was a house in a great neighborhood but in much need of work. At first look, it was a bit difficult to see the potential, but I felt God telling me that this was the house. The price was actually something I could afford with my budget, but because it was in need of so much work, I knew I needed to bring in my trusted friends who had a background with houses. So after a good look and some time in prayer over the home, I decided to take the plunge. We were so grateful to have finally found a home, but there was one catch: the renovations needed for the house had to be done before we could move in and also needed to fit within our tight budget. What's more, we were also on a bit of a tight schedule to move in. Once again, God would have to show up for us in a big way.

Miraculously, one of my dearest friends and her family stepped up to make this overwhelming task happen. They selflessly did everything in their power to help us. We truly could never have done it without them. I wasn't able to do as much since the trauma and grief was still so fresh, yet they cheerfully served me in so many ways throughout the entire renovation. They were so helpful with every task required in pulling this off. Thanks to them, all the renovations were completed right on time.

Finally, we moved into our new home. I have moved many times in my life, but this was a completely different feeling. It was like pulling a ship into the harbor after being out in the roughest of seas. This was a resting place. A place of privacy, stability, and ultimately, a hiding place to heal. We could finally shut out the world a bit and have our own space to process all that we had just been through. Although I still had some big, pressing issues to deal with, they somehow didn't feel quite as overwhelming to me, knowing I had the stability of a home base. We could finally get our things out of storage and slowly try to live more of a normal life, whatever that might look like.

Life started to take shape again. Our dogs finally had a yard to run around and play in, as we previously had no yard for them in the lake house. My kids' friends slowly started to come over to the house as we settled in. I remember thinking how good that felt for my kids to actually have a place for their friends to come over to. It provided a sense of normalcy and stability. Even though there was so much unknown about the future and how our lives were going to play out, we were now able to at least settle in and just live day by day. There was such a sense of gratitude for all that we had, knowing we could have easily had nothing. I was still struggling with God, yet grateful, for I knew it was He that provided the home for us. There was no question that this was a gift from God. My kids and I could now hide and heal for a season.

As wonderful as it was to finally settle into the new home God had provided, it also meant that I was now going to have to deal with all the emotional issues going on inside of me, and it all just seemed too overwhelming. I spent many hours and days curled up in a ball on my bed. This became the safe place I could run to. So many things in my life were uncertain and difficult. I felt so much was still out of my control, and for someone who is a bit of a control freak, this was more than I could handle. I reached a point where the only fight I had left in me was to make sure my kids were taken care of, but beyond that, I was done.

I often felt like I had no capacity to deal with life. Not only did I have to deal with losing my husband suddenly, but adding the element of suicide created an entirely different set of emotions on top of that. There was also the fact that we had to move during all of this trauma and chaos. Put all of those things together and you have yourself one fierce emotional storm.

I remember going to a grief support group at church. Overall, the program was pretty good, and they created a safe place to be able to process death and grief. However, once again, adding the element of suicide into the mix makes it a whole other creature, and I quickly realized that the people in my group couldn't fully relate to my trauma. This made it harder for me to find true support.

One valuable thing I do remember learning in this support group was the one rule they gave us to follow: while in grief, do not get stuck in one place for too long. Another was that they described grief like a ping pong ball bouncing in every direction. This illustrated the fact that there really is no stage-by-stage process for grief, at least not for everyone. Many people who haven't been through grief often think there is a correct way to go through it, as if it's some college course that needs to be followed in a systematic way. They might think that everyone follows the five stages of grief (denial, anger, bargaining, depression, and acceptance) in a linear order. This was not my experience. My emotions were all over the place. What my support group taught me is that for many of us there are no set patterns, no right or wrong ways to handle whatever just shook our world. We are all wired up differently and should not expect everyone to follow a set system when it comes to grief. Understanding this truth helped me to be free from others' expectations and find my own way of grieving through the pain.

Let me just say, sadly, others are too often quick to give their opinion as to how they think you should journey through grief. If you really care about someone going through grief, the best gift and support you can give them is to just be there for them and listen. Do not put expectations on them, as this will often just drive them away from you.

In the midst of these intense and overwhelming emotions, I would find myself curled up in a ball on my bed, picturing myself (in my mind) curled up at God's feet. I wasn't sure how I felt about my relationship with this new God who allowed so much pain. However, I desperately needed to feel safe, and this was the only place that allowed me to feel so. As I moved forward with life, many things would come up that were quite difficult for me to navigate through on my own, and I would quickly run back to His feet, curl up in a ball, and stay in my safe place. For a while though, I only wanted to stay at His feet and not get any closer. Doing so would have required me to work through emotions that I didn't have the energy for.

I can remember thinking, *"Life is probably not going to get much better than this, and there are probably more trials coming, so I will fight for my kids as necessary and then run here to my safe place. At least I might be protected here."* This is really what the Bible refers to as evil foreboding (Proverbs 15:15 AMPC). It's when you start to believe more bad things are coming based on the experiences you have been through. It becomes difficult to believe that the God who allowed so much pain would have anything good for you. After huge trauma, it becomes easier to agree with this thinking, as it appears more logical to the brain. This is what Satan, the enemy, wants us to believe. He loves to try and get us to agree with this when we are hurting, and I was no exception. I accepted the thinking that if I could just keep the kids and I safe then that would have to be good enough. There was no grandiose thinking at this point, just survival. No hope for a better future, just fighting for what was needed, one day at a time.

Chapter 7

I Don't Belong Here Anymore

As I was dealing with the issue of how I now saw God, it was becoming very difficult to go to the church I had known for so long. I had been a part of this church for most of my adult life, where it played a vital part in shaping my family and I's faith. It had become a wonderful place where we did life and community with others. There were so many memories there: baby dedications, baptisms, small groups, serving groups, and funerals. I had met so many wonderful people and lifelong friends in this church. For a long time, it had been home to me.

However, something had changed. It was as if I was seeing church through a completely different lens. I was honestly struggling to see God in a way that would speak to my deep pain. What once was an enjoyable experience was now very difficult. What I now saw were very prepared, polished worship sets and messages that had been meticulously planned and rehearsed. I saw all of the familiar faces and normal church routines, but I wasn't seeing God. At least, I wasn't seeing the God I was looking for.

I am not saying He wasn't there, because I know He was, but I just wasn't feeling His presence. I was looking for the raw, unpolished God. The God who could look me in the eyes and speak directly to my heart. The God who could have those very uncomfortable conversations with me about what had just occurred in my life.

All I experienced were the safe conversations, the ones that were ignoring the elephant in the room. People would ask me how I was doing, whether I was okay, but I could tell they didn't want me to open up too much and wanted to avoid any heavy conversations. I can't blame them. I might do the same in their shoes. This was to no one's fault of their own. I mean, honestly, how in the world would anyone even know where to start with helping me deal with all I had been through? I didn't even know how to help myself. I quickly realized that people are often not equipped to go to those deeper places of pain because they haven't been there. It was unrealistic for me to expect that those around me could possibly know what I was processing or how to help me work through it all.

It quickly became clear to me that I had changed in a dramatic way, while the people around me had not. I needed a God who could go to the dark corners of my heart and speak life back into them. I could no longer survive in an environment with so much predictability. I needed an environment that allowed total freedom: freedom to process anything with God, not just what was on the planner for that week. I couldn't really articulate at the time exactly what I needed. I just knew that I needed something much different from what I had been experiencing for so long.

Please hear me when I say that I mean no disrespect to the church. I believe that God has a specific anointing and calling on this church, which they are fulfilling. There is a huge need for the way they are doing church. Many years ago, it was their specific style of church that drew me in and helped me to come to know God. I would not be where I am today without all of the years spent there. This church had served my family and I well over many years. However, that season had now come to an end.

"To everything there is a season, A time for every purpose under heaven." Ecclesiastes 3:1 (NKJV)

Sadly, this church, which used to bring me so much comfort and life, now felt like a foreign land. I started to lose all desire to go. At first, this felt like a horrible thing. It felt like something was wrong with me. However, I could no longer force myself to go, and interestingly, once I quit going, I had a much greater sense of peace than when I was forcing myself to go. This led me to many conversations with God regarding how He felt about me not wanting to go. Surprisingly, I wasn't feeling the shame or guilt I used to feel when I was away from church for an extended period of time. I wasn't sure if it was only because of what I had just been through, or if there was something bigger going on.

To be perfectly honest, it felt really nice to not force myself to do something that was no longer bringing me any life. Things were hard enough at this point, so trying to force myself to go somewhere I didn't want to go was especially difficult. Even though I was so grateful for the season I had with this church, I knew in my spirit that it was time for a new season with God. I knew that He was so much bigger than the four walls of the church and that I was ready to figure out who He really was. In 2 Corinthians 3:18, the Bible refers to us going from "glory to glory." In other words, God is always wanting to show us more of who He is and wants to bring us to a higher level with Him. For me, that meant it was time to discover God outside of the church walls. So, I settled into a season of discovering God all over again. No guilt. No shame. Just God and I.

After being away from church for a while, Kelly introduced me to some people who had a healing ministry for those who were in deep pain or trauma. Having now stepped away from the church I knew for so long, this ministry was now critical in helping me navigate this new spiritual terrain I was on. It was a safe place to process, under God's protective wings, everything that had happened to me. It was a place where I could look someone in the eye and have a raw, direct conversation about all the pain and trauma I was processing. What really set apart this ministry though was that it was more than just counseling. The couple who ran the ministry strove to bring God's voice into the counseling process. Sometimes they would spend several minutes waiting and listening to hear from the Holy Spirit throughout our sessions. The result was that they would share things with me, and pray things over me, that really spoke to my grieving heart. Often, they would say or pray something that would be totally unrelated to what we had been discussing, but that spoke to something deep in my heart.

It soon became obvious to me that God was often speaking through them. This made my time with them so powerful, as it was ultimately God who knew what I needed. Often, they would speak of my destiny: the destiny that God still had waiting for me regardless of the trauma I had endured. They encouraged me that even though things seemed so bleak in this season, God was going to bring beauty out of all of the pain.

"to strengthen those crushed by despair who mourn in Zion-to give them a beautiful bouquet in the place of ashes, the oil of bliss instead of tears, and the mantle of joyous praise, instead of the spirit of heaviness. Because of this, they will be known as Mighty Oaks of Righteousness, planted by Yahweh as a living display of his glory." Isaiah 61:3(TPT)

This was all new to me. No one had ever spoken into my life this way (other than Kelly). It was powerful. God knew I needed the kind of ministry that would speak life and hope into my weary soul. Up to this point, I had primarily been focused on just surviving and trying to pick up the broken pieces of my life after John's death. This ministry acknowledged the pain and trauma, but then moved into helping me see Heaven's perspective, which brought purpose and clarity to all of the suffering I was enduring. They helped me see that my story had a Kingdom purpose, which was to bring healing to so many others who were suffering. I could feel the love of the Father in every session, and I was desperate to know more about this God: the God who would speak hope over my life in the midst of darkness.

Chapter 8

Better Thoughts

Let me be clear: It is my belief that everything about God should line up with the Bible. Everything that I've learned and continue to learn on my journey must hold up to the teachings of scripture. I fully believe God breathed His breath into the Bible and He will not contradict it. If I come across any particular teaching, or if someone says something that does not match up with the truths of the Bible, I simply dismiss them. So just know as I continue to write about my journey in these further pages, that this is my mindset and my moral compass on everything. As I encounter new people and teachings, I always go back to God's word for clarification.

As I worked with this healing ministry, my eyes were opened to so many new resources and connections. I was introduced to all sorts of churches and ministries that I never knew existed. These were ministries that spoke about a God who focused on calling people higher and speaking life into them, instead of focusing on all the things that people were doing wrong. Have you ever noticed that if you spend all of your time focusing on doing the right things in your life, then you won't really have any time to focus on the negative things? An anonymous quote I have seen often illustrates this principle well: "What you feed will flourish, what you neglect will die." The good things actually push out the bad if there's no time or space for them. My experience with the church, in general, is that there is often so much focus on the areas in people's lives that need to be fixed (all of their shortcomings) before they can truly be used by God. This seemed to keep them in a perpetual cycle of always looking for the next thing that needed to be fixed, instead of focusing on the higher purpose God had for them through the gifts He put inside of them.

Please know that I am a big believer in self-discovery, learning your strengths and weaknesses, your personality types and how you're wired up. I am also a big believer in working through therapy when needed, which can reveal wounds you may not have known were there, to help bring clarity to areas you're struggling with. After all, I have spent many hours in therapy throughout my life, some of which was very helpful. However, similar to my experience with the church, I also noticed that therapy can also build the perpetual cycle of focusing on what's wrong more than what's right. Resting in this cycle for too long can actually keep you from moving forward in God's purpose for your life.

You may be wondering, "What are the good things that I'm supposed to focus on?" One thing you can try for yourself is to pick a powerful statement that speaks to your heart, especially one that is rooted in scripture. For example: "I am fearfully and wonderfully made" (Psalm 139:14)(NIV) Then, meditate on that statement daily. Think about it throughout the day, and maybe speak it out loud when you wake up in the morning and before you go to bed. Think about the wonderful and unique qualities God has given you. Maybe you're a creative, artistic person. Maybe you're a practical, organized problem-solver. Maybe you're very caring and have a huge heart for helping others. Make a list of these different positive qualities, and let it soak in that God has made you this way for a reason. He has given you valuable gifts so that you can bless this world.

Another great thing to try is to send a powerful, encouraging text to someone in your life who is struggling. Think of one thing that would speak life over that person, send it to them each day, and see how it impacts them. The deeper our wounds, the longer it can take for the new words to take root, but they will take root if you're persistent. The beautiful thing is that as you take the time to encourage someone else, just the act of doing so can actually bring you healing and encouragement as well.

I know what I'm saying here might be challenging for some, but it's a powerful concept that needs to be explored more. You see, I had now hit a point in my life where it was really easy to go negative. My family and I had already been through so much with John's death and having to move. There was still so much uncertainty about our future. It was really difficult to see the good God had for us. We were in a stable place, but I was very aware that any new trial could hurl us back into the abyss in a heartbeat. What I began to realize was that there was a subtle message coming through so many people, even within the church, that didn't bring life. It seemed to keep directing my focus only on our negative reality. Things were bleak for us, and the more I would focus on the bad, the less room there was to see or focus on the hope of anything good, let alone great. I desperately needed hope, and not just hope of barely getting by, but hope that there was something amazing out there for me and my family. My focus could no longer be on trying to fix my broken reality, but rather, on embracing God's good gifts for my life.

"For with God nothing shall be impossible." Luke 1:37(KJV)

As I became more aware that there was a new and better way to process my thoughts and how I was seeing my life, it still felt very difficult to break old thought patterns. Especially, since I was still so deeply wounded and heartbroken. Even though God had been showing me new ways to think, it was easier to go back to the old negative ways of thinking, as this was familiar and not requiring any actual effort. This is where my talks with Kelly would become critical to my healing journey. Kelly knew God was asking her to start speaking life into me. Little by little, Kelly would share with me what she saw in the spirit as she prayed for me. God would give her visions of my future.

She even saw me someday telling my story, and here I am telling my story! After everything we had just been through, it seemed even more strange to me that God would have these great things for my future. Each time she would sit and encourage me with what she saw, it would ever so slowly seep into my spirit. Even to this day when we speak, she still encourages me, she still reminds me of the things she sees in the future for my life, and it brings me great hope.

I would find myself looking forward to our time together. I knew she would continue to speak life over me, but even more than that, as I would hit rough spots emotionally, she would hold no judgment. She would just sit with me, allowing me to process whatever came to the surface in that particular moment. The farther I moved through this journey, the messier it became. I had all sorts of emotions, especially towards God. She became one of the few safe places where I could share anything that I was feeling: the big, bad, and ugly stuff that comes up when you are deeply wounded. She knew that God was big enough for everything I was going through, no matter what came out of my mouth. She would just encourage me that God was big enough to handle anything I was feeling.

She even gave me the freedom to be mad at God, which was new to me. This was something I was afraid to let out. One thing I've learned is that religion tells us it's a sin to be mad at God, that it's not okay to even go there. But Christianity is about having a relationship with God, and all healthy relationships require us to be honest about our feelings with the other person. Kelly's encouragement gave me the freedom to actually let that anger out at Him, knowing it would bring me deeper healing and freedom. Without her encouragement, I may have been too afraid to be fully honest with God.

Deep down, I knew I had a big task ahead: to go and deal with all of these rough feelings I had with God. Looking back now, I realize there were several things going on at this time. God knew that I was not in a good place with Him and that I wasn't as open to hearing from Him because of all the pain. He knew that speaking to me through Kelly, whom I deeply trusted, would be a better way for me to hear what He was saying. God was slowly building my hope back up through the words that she would speak over me. This was making me much more willing to work on the deep wounds that needed to be healed, so that I could truly live again.

Without the hope of the future, there would have been no willpower to even deal with these deep wounds. But by giving me a vision for my future, He was giving me the will to fight again. I had no idea how in the world I was going to ever get to those places in the future that He was showing me through Kelly, but now I at least had hope: hope that life could still be beautiful, even after all the devastation.

Chapter 9

The Ugly Nature of Taking Your Life

Back

This was an interesting part of my journey, to say the least. This was not a chapter I was looking forward to writing. I even thought about not putting it in the book, but I knew that wouldn't be honest. I knew that others needed to see the messy process of healing from trauma. It's necessary because this book is really not for me. It's for helping others who might be struggling through difficult circumstances in life, to show the truth of what pain and trauma look like, and for those wanting to learn more of who God truly is in the midst of their pain. So, I felt led by God to include this part of the journey, ugliness and all.

I want to say from the get-go that I am so far from perfect and have made so many mistakes along the way. My emotions were so raw during this season that the ugly side of me really reared its head. I know this ugliness hurt some people in my life. When deep wounds rise to the surface, they, unfortunately, can damage certain relationships around you.

So in the first days, weeks, and even months after John's death, I was just physically and emotionally not able to do all that was needed. I relinquished so much of my life to those around me in order to survive. Without them stepping up and taking the reins, I would not be where I am today. I know that God had placed those people in my life in order for my kids and I to survive. However, there comes a day when you have to take the reins of your life back. This is where it gets messy. There is no training for this. No handbook. No one ever plans to go through this kind of pain. I was in uncharted waters. Slowly, as I regained the ability to think more clearly and start making decisions for my family and myself, I realized that I was in this intense internal battle. The close family and friends I had relied upon and clung to those past few months were now starting to feel like a burden.

Please understand me clearly: they were doing nothing wrong. They had no idea of how to navigate through the mess either. No one had given them a five-step class on how to help someone through all this. They were just these amazing, loving friends who cared deeply about our family. There was no way they could have known all that was going on internally with me. I had just reached a new point where I needed more independence and control back over my life.

As I became more aware of this internal battle, I started trying to find ways of letting those around me know that I was ready to take the reins of my life back. I know I didn't do this very well. Part of me felt guilty because I didn't want anyone to think I wasn't grateful for all they had done, but at the same time I also thought, *"Well maybe they're ready to be done helping me and get back to their own lives?"* So, I moved through this process the best I could. Through all the messiness, most of my friends and family were very gracious and understood that I was moving into a new season. While some of these conversations were awkward, most of them were able to see that this was new territory for me and did not take it personally. I know many of them saw me struggling deep down and just wanted what was best for me.

Looking back now, I realize how truly hard this stage was. Everyone has wounds, and when you put two wounded people together, it's going to get messy; the bigger the wound, the bigger the mess. Sadly, one of my oldest, dearest friends was a casualty of this. There came a point in our relationship during this season where we could no longer move forward together. We hit a brick wall.

First, I tried to explain to her that I was feeling the need to take a period of time to just be alone with God while I worked through some issues that were surfacing. I felt God telling me that this would be best for my healing journey. I needed to take a break from all my friendships for a period of time, so I could just process alone with God and not feel like I had to explain everything that I was working through. I realize that might seem weird to some, but for an introvert, it became a necessity. My friend expressed her concerns that she didn't feel this was a good idea. Honestly, if I would've had the option to go away on a trip by myself and take a sabbatical with God, I would have done so. I think that would have been much easier for people to accept. My spirit desperately needed and wanted time away to work through everything that was rising to the surface. However, this was impossible due to all that was expected of me on a daily basis with caring for my kids. The best I could do was take little moments throughout each day to spend alone time with God.

The truth is that, over the past twenty years, I had developed a good ear to hear God, and I knew when He was speaking to me. I learned that if I didn't obey what He was asking, that I would just have to go around that same mountain again. I did not want to have to stay in this pain any longer than I absolutely needed to.

My friend and I spoke on the phone most days, so I think she was just concerned about there not being someone to check in with me daily. If I lived alone, I could see how this might have been a valid concern. However, I had four teenagers, who I was extremely close with and was always interacting with. She really pushed back, not thinking this was a good idea. I realized from her perspective, it seemed a bit odd, but I was really hoping that she would trust and respect me, knowing that I heard God well. While I appreciated her concern, I knew that it was time for me to go into the wilderness with God.

She and I also disagreed on another issue. You see, the anger I had been feeling towards God had not been dealt with and was starting to rise up. I was wrestling with the fact that I would need to forgive God at some point in order to truly heal. Her particular belief was that God did not need my forgiveness (I will address that issue in a later chapter).

Sadly, the conflict between us only grew, as several other issues also began popping up. Things escalated to the point where she was not willing to talk to me. I was so deeply saddened that this was the point our friendship was at. It was heartbreaking to me that she couldn't understand what I was going through, or at least let me work through it in a way that was best for me. This is where life gets so messy. Every person is wired up differently, and, depending on the personality type, some will be able to work through these issues together and some will not.

My emotions were bubbling up to the surface and I was having a difficult time even trying to understand them myself, let alone explain them to anyone else. The truth about being in a deep place of pain is that the hurt that screams the loudest wins. So as painful as it was to be in such a bad conflict with my friend, the pain of not being right with God was way worse. With nowhere else to go, I went to God. I remember just being so angry at Him with all that was going on. However, the longer I sat talking with Him about the issue, the more I began to feel a wonderful sense of peace come over me and replace the anger. I had not felt that kind of peace for quite some time and was surprised that God would be so gracious with me in all my anger towards Him. The more I quieted myself, the more I could sense Him speaking, and I heard him clearly say in my spirit:

"You are going to need to end this friendship. I am not taking her where I am taking you. Trust Me."

Normally, I might have questioned that, but there was something different about this conversation with God. His peace was resonating deep in my spirit. It was not just some casual conversation with Him. There was a conviction to it. I had a sense that He was saying not only would it be best for me, but for my friend as well. It was one of those times where I knew that I knew what He was saying. Feeling peaceful about ending a friendship may sound harsh to some, but as I've learned to walk with God, He has sometimes asked me to do things that may not make sense to those around me. He helped me to see that because my friend and I were wired up so very differently, it was going to actually cause more pain trying to stay friends. Given everything I had just been through, more pain was something I could not afford to endure.

The truth is, relationships are really important to God. However, He cares more about our relationship with Him over any other relationship in our life. My relationship with Him had become so off course that it was affecting all of my other relationships in a negative way. He knew the healing that was needed in my life, and it needed to start ASAP. Even though God knew how close of a friend she was, and that she had just walked through this entire ordeal with me, He also knew what He had ahead for me and wanted me to walk it alone with Him.

God does not always ask us to end a friendship, but sometimes He does. I have often prayed that God would speak to her heart and let her know that it was He who asked me to walk away. His ways are higher, and He knows best. Sometimes He asks us to do things we may not understand this side of Heaven: even having to walk away from those we love.

Chapter 10

The Wilderness

Up until this point in my journey, things had been, for the most part, overwhelming and hectic. From the moment I received the phone call concerning my husband's death, there was just so much focus on surviving that I never really allowed myself to fully grieve. I would have times of deep sadness and pain, but I would always shut it down and go back into survival mode, focused on providing for my kids and I the basic things we needed: housing, money, and security. Now that God had provided a home, some steady income through Social Security, and the ability to feel somewhat safe and secure, it was time to deal with all of the unfinished business: all of the ugly emotions that were surfacing.

This would become a very long season for me. Much longer than I would have liked. I just wanted to be one of those people who experienced a quick breakthrough with God and moved on. For me though, this wasn't the case.

I was so eager to just go away alone with God for an extended period of time, in hopes of moving through my healing quickly. I can remember before my husband's death how he would allow me to go on a vacation once a year, by myself, to our favorite beach and just spend time with God. I would have great revelations and breakthroughs in my relationship with Him on those vacations. Deep down, I was longing to go do that again. However, there was no way that was going to happen, nor would it have been fair to my kids, as we were all adjusting and all needing each other.

So, the journey into the wilderness began with God and I spending time together every day in between my daily activities. At first, I had no idea where to even start with Him. Most of the time, I wouldn't feel like praying, talking, or reading my Bible. So, I would just sit. It was just Him and I, sitting alone in my room. It felt like I was finally allowing myself to face the truth that I had been stuffing down for a long time. I now had the freedom to allow myself to open up to what had been brewing beneath the surface. I had been seeing pieces of the pain rise up but never allowed it to truly surface. Day after day, I began processing what was going on inside without the fear of judgment from anyone.

At this point, I had no desire to process any of what I was going through with another person. Prior to entering this new wilderness season, I sat in many counseling sessions and spent a lot of time talking with friends and family. I appreciated most of what they shared with me, but I didn't feel total freedom to grieve with them. I needed it to be just God and I for this part of the journey. I am not saying this is the way everyone should deal with their journey of grief, but for me, I had to follow peace, and this was where peace was leading me.

Peace is a wonderful guide to follow when you are unsure if you're in the right place or doing the right thing. I realize that many people are wired up much differently than I am and may need a completely different process for grief. I remember one of the women in my grief support group shared that right after learning of her husband's death, she couldn't stand being alone and needed to have something to do every night. She talked about going to dinners with friends and going to parties as often as she could just to be around people. She shared that she found much more peace when she was around others, and that being alone felt horrible to her. So clearly there is no right or wrong way of moving through grief and pain. I've learned it's crucial to ask God what the best way for you is, and then follow His peace.

For me, I had reached a point where it no longer felt safe to process with anyone but God, and I knew that I had His permission to do so. With Him, I was at least safe to be 100% myself without any judgment. As an introvert, the past season had completely smothered me with little alone time for myself, which was something I especially craved having four kids. Now I could actually breathe and figure out what the heck just happened in my life.

Honestly, I spent months just grieving: grieving without the concern of figuring out how to survive overshadowing everything. As I settled into the rhythm of this grieving process, I allowed anything to come up to the surface that needed to. Since I had spent the past season shoving everything down, everything that was now popping back up felt as though I was seeing it for the first time. I could now fully see the faces of all the hurts and pains I was carrying. They were uninvited guests in my heart that I now had to deal with. It wasn't easy dealing with those uninvited guests, but at some point, they were going to need to leave.

I can remember feeling such deep pain, and thinking to myself, *"If this pain doesn't stop soon, I don't know how I will survive it."* It was in these moments that God would always step in right when I needed it. He would speak to me in different ways. Sometimes, it was through something my kids would randomly say to me. Other times, it was through lyrics in a song that I would hear. He would also speak through verses and quotes I had hung up all over the walls in my room. One of the quotes I had taped to my wall in those days said this:

"God is monitoring the heat of the furnace. He's pouring out the strength that you need, to endure at the moment you feel you can't go on."

It is a James MacDonald quote, which is a paraphrase from Daniel 3:16-19, where three Hebrew men, Shadrach, Meshach, and Abednego were thrown into a fiery furnace by the king, Nebuchadnezzar, but were never burnt. I cannot tell you how many times I looked at and read that quote. It was as if the words jumped right off of the paper and into my heart. It perfectly encapsulated how I was feeling at the time. It brought me incredible comfort to know that God was in fact monitoring the heat of the pain within me. It was as if He was telling me, **"I know this hurts but I will not let it overtake you."**

In between moments of deep grief, I would find myself asking God questions. Questions like: *"Who are you? You're clearly not the God I thought I knew, at least not the God I had neatly packed in a box."* My image of God forever changed on the day of the phone call. You see, I had spent years learning about a God who would always be there for me. I knew there would be trials, as I had experienced many of them already in my journey with Him. However, in my mind, I had a limit for the hardship that He would allow. He clearly did not share that limit. This is where I got tripped up. I was willing to accept a loving God who would be there for me and help me as I encountered the struggles of life. But a God who would allow pain past the limit I had set? This I had not planned for. I thought life was supposed to become easier as I grew in my relationship with God, not harder.

To be perfectly honest, in my mind, I felt like God had crossed the line. This was too much! Life went from being difficult at times to unbearable. I had seen many other people in life walk through horrific traumas, but I never dreamed He would ask me to do the same. I felt like I already had enough struggles in life! With all the hardship I had already faced, I thought, *"God knows! Surely, He would never add more to my plate than I already have. He knows that I have dealt with so much already."*

Next, I would attempt to deal with the "Why" question. Let me just say, He usually doesn't answer this one. I wanted to say that He never answers it, but that would be putting Him in a box (something I don't do anymore). To address this as simply as possible, my experience with this question is that His ways are higher and often we are not able to fully understand them. The Bible tells us that we understand in part but are not given the whole picture. This is why faith is so vitally necessary to fully walk with God. There is an element of trusting that He knows best and we do not.

"For now we see but a faint reflection of riddles and mysteries as though reflected in a mirror, but one day we will see face-to-face. My understanding is incomplete now, but one day I will understand everything..." 1 Corinthian 13:12 (TPT)

This also might be a good place to explain something about God that I have not shared up until this point: My husband's death was not God's will.

He didn't want it to happen. My experience with God is that He doesn't cause or orchestrate trauma, but the enemy does!

"A thief has only one thing in mind—he wants to steal, slaughter, and destroy. But I have come to give you everything in abundance, more than you expect—life in its fullness until you overflow! I am the Good Shepherd who lays down my life as a sacrifice for the sheep." John 10:10-11 (TPT)

I love what Bill Johnson, pastor of Bethel Church, has to say on this subject: "There's no question that God can turn any situation around for His glory and our benefit - this of course includes the most evil conditions known to humanity around the world. But that is the testimony of His greatness and His redemptive purpose. It does not represent His design... It's not complicated. Loss, death and destruction are the things left behind when the devil has had influence in a certain situation. Jesus is the *Good* Shepherd. And what does that goodness look like? He gives abundant life." I know this is a tough one for some to wrestle with. Believe me when I say that I wrestled with this one for quite some time. Through much prayer and time spent with God, He made it clear to me that He was just as heartbroken as I was for the pain our family has endured. Truth is, we live in a world of good and evil. Everyone has free will to make whatever choices they so choose. There is also a spiritual battle going on between good and evil that plays out over the whole of creation, including each of our lives. Pain is allowed, making us feel as though certain battles are lost. However, from God's perspective, He can use anything and everything to win the war. In fact, He's already won the war thanks to Jesus' death and resurrection. Someday we will see the fullness of that victory. Everything will be made right on the day when Heaven and Earth become one.

"He will wipe away every tear from their eyes and eliminate death entirely. No one will mourn or weep any longer. The pain of wounds will no longer exist, for the old order has ceased."

Revelation 21:4 (TPT)

Unfortunately, even though God had helped me to understand that, like me, He was heartbroken over John's death, I still couldn't help but keep asking Him, *"Why did you allow it when You could have intervened?"* Although I eventually learned this was a fruitless question to ask, I spent a while going around this mountain with Him. I just kept asking Him, *"But it would have been so easy for you to step in and stop this? John prayed every morning with You, seeking Your help with all of the struggles we were facing, but You didn't stop it?"* No matter how many times I asked these sorts of questions, I still wouldn't get any answers. This, honestly, was one of the biggest hurdles for me to get over. It really took time. Instead of answering the question, He would gently show me scriptures about how He was there with me in the pain. For instance, Psalm 68:5 was one that spoke to my heart deeply:

"A Father to the fatherless, A defender of widows, Is God in his holy dwelling." (NIV)

The Passion translation says it this way:

"To the Fatherless he is a father. To the widow he is a champion friend." (TPT)

I particularly like the way the Passion translation states this verse, as I so needed a champion friend! To this day, I still cling to this truth, helping me to know that He hasn't left me, and He knows everything I am going through.

Even though my spirit knew that God was there with me in the pain and grief, my emotions started rearing their ugly head. I think I was getting mad that God wasn't answering my questions, at least the way I wanted Him to. Although He was comforting me, He wasn't giving me what I wanted. I had allowed grief to regress myself to that of a two-year-old. My emotions were taking the driver's seat, and I was now entering a new stage.

I was so brokenhearted and angry over the way my life was going (or not going) and I wanted God to know it. More and more anger started to rise up as my flesh was taking over, and I decided to let God know that I was unsure whether I could do things His way anymore. I was dealing with the reality of how hard it was to be a widow and raise four teenagers into adulthood. This was a time when I really needed my husband's help in so many ways; a time when my kids really needed their dad. It was so painful for me to watch. What's more, things were getting harder and harder in regard to my financial situation. There were so many needs and I could not possibly handle them all on my own.

One day, I finally told God I'd had enough. Even though He had been there with me in the pain, showing Himself to me in so many ways, my feelings were now taking over. I simply told Him that I was done and wanted to just go my own way. I can remember telling him things like, *"If this is your plan, it sucks!" "You're supposed to be this big great God, and this is the best you have for me?"* The list goes on and only gets worse. Honestly, I knew deep down that this was stupid, but I just didn't care. My feelings were so raw, and I felt like I needed to take it out on someone. So, God was the best option.

Day after day, I tried desperately to escape into whatever was most comforting: food, watching a lot of TV (which is a great way to escape), and trying to figure out a way to make enough money to fix my situation. Basically, I was trying to solve my own problems without God. As you might guess, this phase didn't go very well. If I had not known a life with God, I could have probably stayed in this season for a long time, but for me, that wasn't going to work. You see, I had learned to live in a place of peace as much as possible. So the more I pulled away from God, the less peace I would have.

However, my anger with Him was so great that I chose to allow myself to stay in that very uncomfortable place for much longer than I should have. I was hoping this would somehow prove a point to God. It was stupid, I know, but I think at some level I wanted to teach God a lesson. My thought was something like *"Well God, you really did it this time. You pushed me away for good. Are you happy now?"* In my head, I can hear some people gasping as they read this. However, I was in such deep pain at this point. It was not a great place to be, but it was real and honest. No matter how angry I became though, He never left my side. He was big enough to take it all.

As my spirit started to come back into the picture and take some control over my flesh, the anger began to subside, and I started experiencing deep remorse and sadness over how I had treated God. I began beating myself up for the things I had said to Him in my pain and how I had tried shutting Him out of my life. Much like a toddler having tantrums in hopes of getting my way, when I came down from the anger, I was exhausted and had little energy left to fight. So, I reluctantly surrendered, and God now had something to work with. Honestly, He was so patient with me during my little season of tantrums, never punishing me, and always so gracious with me. He knew it all just needed to come out. After much time spent in repentance, apologizing to God for my behavior, I began to feel peace setting back in. Balance and order were now coming back into my emotional life.

God now had my attention. As His peace began to take over in the wake of all the pain and anger, I began to realize that the wilderness might not be as bad as I had originally thought. While I still had unanswered questions, I felt the way many do after a good cry: tired, but with a strange sense of relief. I didn't realize it at the time, but God was showing me that I could, in fact, trust Him. He had allowed me to be an absolute idiot in His presence for a short season, yet never condemning me, and still loving me with mercy and grace the whole way through. I am not sure another human would have been so gracious with me. The idea of a God who would allow such disrespect to be let out was new to me. I could actually be completely honest with Him, while being perfectly loved by Him.

While repentance was necessary, it was as if He was reestablishing a new relationship with me, so that deep healing could occur. God will meet each one of us where we are, and deal with us as individuals in the way He sees best. It is important to not put God in a box and say that He will interact with each one of us in the exact same manner because often He won't.

In a weird way, that I can't fully explain, I began to somehow enjoy this peaceful place in the wilderness, as I now had a small sense of hope again. God was, after all, rebuilding my trust and giving me a reason to pursue more of Him. While this was a beautiful time and season with God, things did not improve with Him quickly. The truth is, this was a long season (years) of rediscovering God. It was peaceful, but it definitely took time. One of the verses hanging on my wall at the time read:

"When they walk through the Valley of Weeping, it will become a place of refreshing springs, where pools of blessing collect after the rains" (Psalm 84:6) (NLT).

Great relationships take time to develop, and my relationship with God was no exception. As time progressed, my heart would heal more and more, but my circumstances remained difficult for a long time. My finances were stretched tight, and my children were experiencing different challenges in their own lives. I had to deal with both of these issues without the help of my husband. As I look back now, I can see that God was using those difficult issues for a season, as they kept me drawing closer to Him. The difficulties, on top of the grief, kept me in a place of total reliance on God. If everything in my life had been going well, besides having the grief to deal with, I might have been tempted to keep God at an arm's length, and not pursue a deeper relationship with Him, missing out on the deeper things He had for me. However, with so many issues being too big for me to handle on my own, it kept me running back to God.

A new struggle started surfacing. Even though I had no doubt that John was in Heaven and out of pain, I was struggling with the fact that I didn't get to talk to him before he left. I was so sad he was gone. I had been crying to God, asking for some kind of sign. I didn't even really know what I was asking for. I just missed talking with John. I missed the phone ringing for our afternoon chats that we would have each day. I didn't like doing life without my best friend. That was the hardest part. It was just so final. When he died, we still had so much more of life to live together here on Earth. It felt too long having to wait to see him in Heaven someday.

One day, I was outside in the backyard with our dogs. I was standing on the patio talking with God, and as I looked down, I noticed a small piece of white cardboard amongst the leaves. I reached down to pick it up, thinking it was just some garbage in the yard, but as I looked closer, I saw that there were words on it. It simply read, "Miss you, I'm sorry." I starting crying, as I knew this was in fact the sign from God I had been praying for: a message that He allowed from John. It was a small message, but incredibly important to me. It was a confirmation that God understood my pain and knew that a simple note from Heaven would speak directly to my heart. Some might be tempted to say it was just a coincidence, but with God there are no coincidences. It was God, once again, showing Himself to me in my pain. My prayer was answered, and I was able to hear one last message from my best friend.

Now that I had settled into this season of the wilderness, I was better equipped to process with God in a healthier way. I could now go back to those questions rolling around in my head. Foremost, was the question, *"If You allowed this, what else will You allow?"* This was a perfectly acceptable question to me, as I felt completely blindsided by all that had occurred. It only seemed fair to ask so I could be more prepared for what might come next. Once again, I quickly discovered that God was not going to answer this question either. He was more interested in building my faith to trust Him no matter what came my way in life.

Remember earlier, when I was talking about evil foreboding? Well, in all honesty, I was still struggling with suspicious thoughts that there were probably more bad things coming my way. I didn't want to think in this way, but it just kinda kept creeping back up. This was a result of the deep heartache I was still experiencing. God showed me, over time, that it was actually my way of putting up a wall: a defense mechanism. By expecting more bad things to happen, then I wouldn't be surprised when they did. This is a very dysfunctional way of thinking, but at the time, it made perfect sense to my broken heart. The problem with this line of thinking is that I was never opening myself up to the good stuff. Not expecting anything good to happen is a very depressing way to live. So, God gently went back to work on the dysfunctional thinking that I was still struggling with.

First, He would show me through Bible verse after Bible verse that He did, in fact, have good plans for my life, regardless of what had happened up until this point. This was difficult for me to grasp, as I just kept going back to all the bad things that had just happened. This, however, was my problem. I kept looking back, but God wanted me to look forward. I wanted to hold on to the pain, but God wanted me to see the blessings He had waiting for me ahead. A part of me didn't want to let go of the pain, as somehow I felt that I had earned it in a weird way. It was almost like it was some award I had earned from going through this horrific trauma. If I let go of the pain and trauma, where would that leave me? Who would I be then? At least if I stayed the poor widow, I'd have something to cling to. Even though I didn't like that title, it was at least something I could claim as mine.

I remember sitting in a counseling session with a very trusted counselor who I had been working with since the beginning of my ordeal. He once said to me, "Karen, it's like you have been away at war and you're now returning home, but it's difficult to just go back to having a normal life. Nothing is the same for you. Everything has changed since you left for war, and you can't go back to the life you once knew. You have a completely different outlook on life and have to rediscover who you are." So, here I was, trying to figure out who the heck I was now? I didn't know how to do that. I didn't even know where to begin. This was a very vulnerable and scary place for me. I really didn't want to rediscover myself at the age of 48, but I really didn't have a choice.

Little by little, God would show me verses like:

"I will lead the blind by ways they have not known, along unfamiliar paths I will guide them; I will turn the darkness into light before them and make the rough places smooth. These are the things I will do; I will not forsake them." Isaiah 42:16 (NIV)

"I will go before thee, and make the crooked places straight." Isaiah 45:2 (KJV)

"'For I know the plans I have for you', declares the Lord, 'plans to prosper you and not to harm you, plans to give you a hope and a future.'" Jeremiah 29:11 (NIV)

"For I am the Lord, your God, who takes hold of your right hand and says to you, Do not fear; I will help you." Isaiah 41:13 (NIV)

I would tape these up on my walls so that I could let them soak into my spirit. One verse that was very special to me at the time would have to be John 6:12 (AMPC) which read:

"gather up for now the fragments (the broken pieces that are leftover), so that nothing may be lost and wasted."

This verse spoke right into the deep places of my heart once again. It was as if God was saying that He saw every pain in my heart, big and small, and that He was not going to waste any of it. Although He didn't cause it, He would use it all for a purpose. It brought me hope that somehow God would take this horrible trauma and make something good out of it.

Another powerful scripture God gave me was Isaiah 61:1-3, which reads:

"The Spirit of the Sovereign Lord is on me… He has sent me to bind up the brokenhearted… to comfort all who mourn, and provide for those who grieve in Zion - to bestow on them a crown of beauty instead of ashes." (NIV)

Beauty for ashes. That was something I desperately needed. I had a lot of ashes! Although I had no idea how God would make beauty out of my ashes, it still brought me a level of hope. He was gently calling me higher to see the heavenly picture. I was slowly starting to accept the fact that my life was not going to be what I had planned, but that at least God was going to make something beautiful from it. What really started happening at this point was that I started to focus on other people in the world who were hurting, who were experiencing deep pain. I started to think that maybe God would use me to help others in their pain. It started to dawn on me that this was maybe my Kingdom purpose. Maybe life was not about me, but rather what I could do for others with God working through me. Maybe, somehow, I could bring comfort to others, as I would be able to relate to their deep pain. Maybe

I could guide them to a God who loves them in the midst of their pain and will make beauty from their ashes.

Even though God had been slowly rebuilding my trust with Him, I still felt the lingering question: *"How can I really trust you?"* God had shown me more of His character and that He had good plans for my future, but for some reason, this question still lingered. I can remember Kelly telling me that she had a vision of me walking around the edge of a pool and that God was in the pool asking me to jump into His arms. However, in the vision, I was reluctant, only dipping my toes in the water, but not wanting to jump. As I pondered her words, I was keenly aware of how accurately this illustrated my relationship with God.

For a long season, I struggled with fully trusting Him again. Although I had made a lot of progress, I clearly had more work to do. It wasn't as if I didn't trust Him at all. I did, but there was something holding me back. I continued to move forward in my relationship with God, but I was still very cautious.

Chapter 11

A Work in Progress

Now that I was finally making some progress with God, I was eager to learn more. I was introduced to a wonderful little house of prayer. It was a place where you could go and soak in live worship music most days of the week. It was also a place where you could go and receive prayer for any need you might have. It was a safe place to just sit in God's presence and process life. My kids and I had started going there to receive SOZO healing prayer, which was helping us learn how to listen more closely to God's voice and what He might be saying as we prayed. Our hope was to gain a better understanding for all we had been through and how to move forward in life.

We met with a precious woman named Julie. She's someone who, once you're in her presence, you never want to leave. She is so full of peace and joy! She quickly became someone I would look to for guidance and direction, as she had a wonderful way of helping me sort through life. I had never learned how to truly see what Heaven sees. I had been ministered to in this way while working with the healing ministry but had not learned how to hear Heaven's perspective for myself. I have often heard the phrase, "Have a heavenly perspective," or, "you need to see what God sees." But I didn't know how to pray in a way that would allow me to see God's perspective at a deeper level. I had learned how to listen for God speaking to my spirit over the years, and I felt that I heard Him well, but I hadn't yet learned how to pray in a way that would bring greater revelation over my life. At a simple level, I could see how God might be viewing a certain situation, but I had never gone to a deeper level with Him to truly access a genuine heavenly perspective.

When I first started working with Julie, she would teach me how to sit and wait on God. We would pray and invite God into our prayer and into our conversation, and then we would just wait on Him. Now, although I had always known how important it was to listen for God to speak after praying, this was a bit different. We would always start by asking God to give us an image in our mind of how He was with us. Every time would be different, as God is very creative. Sometimes He would show me images of us walking on the beach together (something I loved doing with Him), but sometimes we would be dancing, swinging on a swing together, or maybe skydiving! The whole point of this was to help establish a point of connection with God, so that we could start to interact with Him and be aware of what He might want to show or say to us. If you truly wait on Him, He will show you all sorts of things. This is His way of connecting with you on a personal level. This was very helpful for me because I no longer felt like I was just talking to a God somewhere high in the sky.

When I first began to try this type of prayer, I wondered if I was just making things up with my own imagination. Then God reminded me that it was He who created my imagination! The second step was to ask Him what He wanted to speak to me about. This is where He would often show me another image of something that He wanted to draw my attention to. This is a very personal process and is different for everyone.

Initially, it took me a while to learn how to truly relax and just wait on God to speak. After practicing this type of prayer a few times, I started to get the hang of it. It helped to realize on a deeper level that God is very personal and truly wants to connect with all of us in a deeply personal way. This was very helpful for me because even though I knew God was with me, I often didn't feel His presence, and felt so alone much of the time. To learn how to sit with Him and connect in this new way allowed me to feel His presence more of the time. The more I practiced this the more He would show me things and bring greater understanding to issues in my life.

"Call to me and I will answer you. I'll tell you marvelous and wondrous things that you could never figure out on your own."
Jeremiah 33:3 (MSG)

Through Julie, I would learn of so many other connections. It opened up doors to things like worship nights, prophetic conferences, miracle services, healing ministries and so much more.

One of the first worship nights I went to was hosted by this house of prayer. It was like nothing I had ever experienced before. This was not your typical planned-out worship set with a list of songs that had been fully rehearsed ahead of time. It was Holy Spirit led, with amazing musicians who knew how to wait on the Holy Spirit for direction. However the Holy Spirit would lead, that's where the worship would go. The more the night went on, the more heavenly worship became. I can remember feeling at points like I was actually experiencing a piece of Heaven. I was truly getting to feel God's presence. I can remember thinking to myself, *"This is the God I have been looking for. This is real, and it moves my spirit."*

Something I remember noticing was that no one in the room was concerned about anyone else. They were all focused on connecting with God at a deeper level through worship. Some people were happy and dancing, some were sitting quietly on the floor, some were lying face down on the floor, and other people just sat in chairs. There was no expectation, no particular order, just worship in its purest and most genuine form. This was all so new to me, and there was definitely an element of discomfort since this was all so different from what I was used to. I wasn't always sure what to expect, but because I felt God's presence, I wanted to press in and know more. God was showing me what the next level of worship looked like. He helped me to realize that although the long season I had previously been in was necessary for my journey, it was now time to go higher. He wanted me to experience His presence at a deeper level, in order to bring the healing that was needed in my life.

I began to go to more Holy Spirit-led worship events at different places and kept noticing that most of the people attending were full of joy. I mean, really full of joy! Like in a way I had never seen before. Don't get me wrong, there were others there that were more like me, hurting from trauma and looking for a healing touch from God. However, my focus seemed to stay on all the people full of this new joyous life.

"for the joy of the Lord is your strength." Nehemiah 8:10 (NIV)

They would dance with no shame and sing loudly no matter how they sounded. If I had seen something like that in my previous church days, everyone in the church would have been embarrassed for that person dancing and singing with joy, so it was challenging for me at first. I had to shut down those old thoughts that I have now come to know as a "religious spirit." I'm referring to thoughts like, *"You can sing but not too loud. You can maybe dance a little, but not to the point of bringing attention to yourself. Church has to be orderly and you must follow a system."* All of these thoughts stemmed from what religion had taught me, but I began to discover they really weren't from God.

Something I find funny is that it's so acceptable to go crazy at a football game and no one thinks twice about it, but if you go crazy in joy and worship, dancing before the Lord who created the universe, you're considered out of line. Interesting, don't you think? The beautiful thing about this new atmosphere I was experiencing was that nobody really cared what anyone else was doing. There was freedom from any judgment. Once I was able to accept that it was really ok to just be myself, and that others were not concerned about how I chose to worship God, that it was in fact just God and I in the midst of others doing the same, I was finally able to experience freedom with God like never before. This was exactly what my spirit needed; just to be a child of God, dancing carelessly before my Father. Every time I was able to freely dance in His presence as His daughter, I was able to leave behind the identity of the grieving widow who was angry at God. Slowly, God was bringing me into my new identity.

As I recall my journey through this season, the thing that stands out the most is how patient God was with me in terms of learning how to have better thoughts about my life. I had learned so much on this topic and yet, at times, still struggled to actually do it. God would just keep reminding me to go back to what I had learned. He would often remind me through scriptures like Isaiah 55:8-9:

"For my thoughts are not your thoughts, nor are your ways my ways," declares the Lord. "For as the heavens are higher than the earth, so are my ways higher than your ways and my thoughts higher than your thoughts." (AMP)

It was clear that God was not going to give up on teaching me how to speak life over myself. Little by little, it was slowly allowing me to change my thoughts of doom and gloom to thoughts like, *Maybe God does really have something good for me. Maybe even something great for me.* It was not a quick process. It took daily effort and mindfulness to think like this. However, I noticed more and more that this positive thinking was keeping me from going to the dark places that I was so tempted to go in the season prior.

All that I had been learning over the past few years was finally starting to take root. God was also really driving home that the words I speak really matter. I felt Him saying it was time to get really serious about every word that came out of my mouth. I now had to catch myself when I was tempted to go back to old ways of thinking, which would cause me to speak negatively about myself or my situation. He wanted me to see that speaking negative words over my life was not going to help me get to where I wanted to go.

"Words kill, words give life; they're either poison or fruit—you choose." Proverbs 18:21 (MSG)

As I continued speaking scriptures over my life, and the lives of my kids, I could feel a strength building within me. I am still growing in this area all the time.

One weekend, when I was attending a prophetic conference, my friend Julie, who was helping run the conference, suggested that I receive some ministry (prayer). She knew I was struggling with some issues and feeling a bit stuck in my journey at that point. So, she asked some friends of hers, who were there to prophesy over people, if they would sit with me and pray. They graciously agreed.

Now let me clear the air for those who might be uncomfortable with the idea of receiving prophetic words or anyone who has a false sense of what prophecy is. Prophecy is, at its core, prayer. That's it. It's prayer. It might be helpful to think of it as reverse-prayer. Most of us have the idea that prayer is us speaking to God. Prophecy is the opposite: it's God speaking to us. It's learning how to pray to God and then waiting on Him to see if He has a message for a particular person. Sometimes it requires much patience and listening for God to speak. Sometimes He doesn't speak. A true prophet will only speak if and when he or she hears God's heart on a matter. A true prophet will not speak anything other than what God gives them. True prophecy should only ever encourage and comfort those receiving the prophetic word. It also should never contradict the Bible.

"But when someone prophecies, he speaks to encourage people, to build them up, and to bring them comfort."
1 Corinthians 14:3 (TPT)

"No true prophecy comes from human initiative but is inspired by the moving of the Holy Spirit upon those who spoke the message that came from God." 2 Peter 1:21 (TPT)

Unfortunately, there are some that have been wounded by prophetic words that didn't come from God. This, sadly, has given this spiritual gift a bad name. I recently heard Bill Johnson say, "that anything of value will often have counterfeits." Prophecy is no exception. There is also the fact that there are many people who are immature in prophecy and still learning how to do it. This obviously leaves room for error. However, there are many people in God's Kingdom who operate in the prophetic gift in an accurate and powerful way that brings life. I have witnessed many people who have received life-giving prophecies and watched how it literally brought life back into them.

While I believe it is always best to go directly to God first for every matter in my life, there are also times when I really welcome a word from someone who hears God well. This can help bring confirmation to something

I think I might be hearing or bring deeper clarity on a matter. I am however, very careful who I receive prophecy from. If I decide to receive a word from someone, I will always hold it up to the Bible, making sure there is nothing spoken over my life that would contradict God's truth. If it isn't from God, then I don't want anything to do with it.

I realize I may have opened a can of worms for some with this topic. However, this is a part of my journey. I have healed so much through this type of ministry that I wouldn't be doing this book justice if I left it out.

With that clarified, let's jump back to the women who prayed and prophesied over me. I had been sitting with them for about a good forty-five minutes. As we sat, they shared things with me about my life that they could have never known on their own. I had never met them before, yet they were sharing things about my life that were so accurate. As they prayed for me, God was showing them things in the spirit that He wanted me to know. Much of what they spoke was lining up with what my friend Kelly had been speaking over me throughout the years prior. This was clearly God encouraging me that I was on the right path, and that He did in fact have so much more for me to accomplish in my life. Without going in to all of the details of what they spoke over me, let's just say that I clearly knew it was very much from God. It gave me more and more hope for the future, breaking away the darkness that had tried to surround me. Although it took several years, this was one of the ways that God confirmed that He wanted me to write this book.

That is the simple purpose of prophecy: to encourage, build up and bring comfort. God knows how difficult it can be doing life here on Earth, as well as learning how to partner with an invisible God. Personally, I am so grateful for all of the gifts of the spirit, including prophecy. While it took some time to understand and become comfortable with, if it hadn't been for this path of prophetic healing, I'm not sure where I'd be at in my journey today.

"When there is no clear prophetic vision, people quickly wander astray. But when you follow the revelation of the word, heaven's bliss fills your soul." Proverbs 29:18 (TPT)

"Lord, direct me throughout my journey so I can experience your plans for my life. Reveal the life-paths that are pleasing to you. Escort me along the way; take me by the hand and teach me. For you are the God of my increasing salvation; I have wrapped my heart into yours!" Psalm 25:4-5 (TPT)

Chapter 12

Forgiving God

What I originally thought would be a one-time event, some sort of supernatural moment where I finally came to a place of true forgiveness for all the pain and trauma that God allowed in my life, was to my surprise, something completely different. As I sat and began talking with Him about writing this chapter, He brought more clarity to my journey of forgiveness with Him. He allowed me to realize that my journey of forgiveness was, in fact, a journey and a process.

Let me back it up a bit to paint a better picture for you. In the earlier days of my journey, when I first became aware of my need to forgive God for the anger I was carrying towards Him, I would find myself feeling so guilty about even having that anger. I would just sit and tell Him how sorry I was and that I did forgive Him. However, I wouldn't necessarily feel like anything had changed, and it wouldn't take long before my feelings of anger rose back up. So while I would say the words, my feelings would not actually catch up.

Throughout the wilderness journey, there were many times when I would revisit this anger, telling God that I wanted to forgive Him, but never actually feeling that genuine forgiveness had taken place. While progress was made with each round of forgiveness, it still wasn't addressing the root of my anger, which was ultimately the obstacle holding me back from being able to fully forgive God. It was like the onion effect, layer by layer, slowly forgiving Him, but always with more layers to go. Even before the death of my husband, there were many other trials I had been through (which could fill a whole book in itself). The pain from my husband's death had brought up the pain from these previous trials as well. All of this pain had left deep layers of anger towards God.

Anyone who has ever studied the topic of forgiveness knows that the purpose of forgiveness is not for the person receiving it, but for the person choosing to do the forgiving. This act, when done with the right heart, is to release the person doing the forgiving from staying trapped in unforgiveness and bitterness. The person being forgiven may also benefit from this, but the heart of forgiveness rests in the person who chooses to forgive.

According to the pastor and theologian R.T. Kendall, "We must forgive those on the earth who have hurt us, and we must forgive God in heaven who lets hurtful things happen. In much the same way as we experience peace when we totally forgive those who have hurt us, so too when we come to the place where we totally forgive God." He also goes on to say: "When we don't forgive God, this will almost certainly have a negative effect on our relationships with people. Very likely, we will have a problem forgiving them for their wrongs. Bitterness will be the consequence of unforgiveness"

Some people might have anger towards God and be able to forgive Him in one prayer and feel total freedom. However, for my journey, God was wise and patient enough to allow my process to take as long as it needed to take. We are all different. Our journeys are all different. Our deep hurts and pains are all different. So forgiving God may look different for each of us. He knew that my pain ran deep. So, for me to just be able to forgive Him in one single prayer would have meant not dealing with all my layers of pain. So day-by-day, month-by-month, and year-by-year, He was patient, gently showing me more of whom He truly was and that I could trust Him in the process no matter how long it took. He didn't just want a small part of my heart to forgive Him, He wanted my whole heart.

God knew all along that He never needed my forgiveness, but He knew how critical it was for me to genuinely release the forgiveness so that I could truly be free! Free from caring around the weight of unforgiveness (something I was never meant to carry). Free to live the life that He had waiting for me. Free to fully live again. There is nothing we can release to God that He isn't big enough to handle. Whether it's a struggle we face, or even needing to forgive Him, He can take it all.

You might ask how I knew when I had fully forgiven God. Well, I reached a point in my journey where a good amount of healing had taken place and I was finally able to get to the root of my pain. There were actually several things I discovered about myself as I was digging deep. First, I had buried a feeling, a belief actually, that I was not good enough. It most likely was something I came into agreement with as a child and kept it stuffed down deep throughout my life. At the same time, I realized that fear had been in the driver's seat for a long time. This was not your average fear that was visible to others. It was much more controlled. Much more subtle. Lurking behind every area of my life; behind every decision I made. Its power was not to be underestimated in its control over me. This fear didn't want to relinquish control to a God who had allowed so much pain.

The feeling that I wasn't good enough had been the catalyst which allowed fear in. Fear quickly built a wall to keep all perceived threats out in hopes of protecting myself from pain. All of the trauma I have endured thus far in my life only reinforced the need for the wall. This was not going to allow any true healing to occur. I realized that I needed to allow God into the deep places of my wounded heart. By keeping my wall up, I was keeping God at a distance. Revelation 3:20 (TPT) states it like this:

"Behold, I'm standing at the door, knocking. If your heart is open to hear my voice and you open the door within, I will come in to you and feast with you, and you will feast with me."

The truth is that God will never force His way into your heart, or the broken places in it, He must be invited. He gives you free will in every area of your life. He deeply desires to have an intimate relationship with you, but only if you first invite Him in. You can ask Jesus into your life, to be your savior, but still deny Him access to wounded areas deep within you. Take the image of a house with many rooms. You may invite Him into the living room and the kitchen but deny Him access into all of the other rooms of your house. While you are still saved, because Jesus is living in your heart, you are not experiencing the full freedom He wants to give you. As you walk with God, you should always be asking Him to seek your heart and show you the areas where you need healing so that you can move into greater and greater levels of freedom. God will never force this healing; it is up to you to decide how much you are willing to allow Him access.

Truthfully, I was protecting myself from a God I was afraid to fully trust. I was afraid that He would just allow even more pain. However, I came to a point where I understood that although He allowed the pain in my life, He certainly didn't cause it. In fact, through some of my SOZO prayer, I saw that He was grieving with me in my pain.

"The Lord is close to the brokenhearted and saves those who are crushed in spirit." Psalm 34:18(NIV)

"He always comes alongside us to comfort us in every suffering so that we can come alongside those who are in any painful trial. We can bring them the same comfort that God has poured out upon us." 2 Corinthians 1:4 (TPT)

"When Jesus looked at Mary and saw her weeping at his feet, and all her friends who were with her grieving, he shuddered with emotion and was deeply moved with tenderness and compassion." John 11:33 (TPT)

I came to the realization that He had been showing me that He was never going to leave my side, no matter how long it took me to come to a place of allowing Him access into the wounded places of my heart. He patiently allowed me my process of going to the dark corners of my pain, as He continued to show His deep love for me. He then allowed me to see that life with Him was way better than without Him.

Through the prophetic words spoken to me, He also showed me that He had good things in store for my future. While I will most likely encounter more pain in my lifetime, I came to the realization that I only wanted to face it all with Him. No walls, no fear, just trust. So brick by brick we tore that wall down together.

Forgiveness, for me, was the key to freedom, and I'd much rather be free than stuck behind a wall of false safety.

Chapter 13

The West Calls

"God told Abram: 'Leave your country, your family, and your father's home for a land that I will show you.'"

Genesis 12:1 (MSG)

Starting a new season is something that can be both difficult and wonderful. Some seasons can be especially difficult, like the journey shown so far in this book, while others can be much more exciting. However, they are often a mix of both. Eventually, it was time once again for a new season. God was asking me to say goodbye to our healing home in Illinois and embrace a season of adventure in California. Although I was very excited to say goodbye to a season of so much pain, it also meant saying goodbye to my family and lifelong friends; the land I had lived in my whole life. This was the place where I had grown up and become so familiar with. It was the only real home I had ever known in my lifetime. So this new season, although exciting, had some sadness attached to it.

Leaving my mom would prove to be the most difficult part of all. While we lived far enough away that we didn't see each other all of the time, knowing I could get in the car and be at her house in under an hour was always a comforting feeling, no matter how old I was. The truth is, my mom has been one of my biggest blessings in life. She has always been there for me, no matter what season I've been in, never judging, and only ever believing the best for me. Even through the really difficult days, she always made sure I knew that she was there for me, that she had my back, and that she was never going to leave me. I knew I could always go to her for help no matter what I was going through. The older I have gotten, the more I have come to realize what an amazing mother I have been blessed with.

However, saying goodbye to Illinois, the land I had become so familiar with, was not difficult at all. Truthfully, so many places just felt like a constant reminder of the life I no longer had. That life was gone and never coming back. It actually became a relief to say goodbye to the places that had become so familiar. There was more hope in a fresh start somewhere new without all of the reminders. This hope would prove to be crucial, as God asked us to sell most of our things, keep only what was really important, and move to California without knowing how it was all going to work out.

So, you might ask, "How did you know that God was asking you to sell almost everything and move across the country to Southern California? All while having no idea where you would live?" Well, let me backup for a minute (again). God had been planting seeds for a few years prior. There were so many ways He spoke to me concerning this move. Some of the ways were very easy to figure out, as He was making living in Illinois less and less comfortable. I was starting to really dislike the weather much of the time. There was so much cold and lack of sun throughout the winters. I would find myself really struggling emotionally more and more through the winter. This made me realize my love for the sun and how I felt so infinitely better when I could be in it on a daily basis.

Another way was He spoke was through my son, Luke, who studies Jiu-Jitsu. This was several years prior to our actual move, but God gave him a thought about training in Southern California. Luke then felt strongly that we should go visit and try a particular Jiu-Jitsu school out there. So, him and I took a trip out there to see what we'd find. We spent several weeks there, and I know God was planting the seeds. It was clear from that trip that we really wanted to live out there. We originally thought that a move would happen quickly, but God's timing is not always our timing.

God also often spoke to my oldest son, J.T., who had learned to look for signs from Him. He would show my son California symbols in a variety of ways, almost to a ridiculous level. God really has such a sense of humor and would often show J.T. signs in really funny ways. Not only did He speak to us about the move to California, but about any subject. One time, we were driving on the highway, talking about wanting to start eating healthier, needing more vegetables in our diet, and at that exact moment, a produce truck pulled up right next to us with pictures of life-size vegetables, all which had big smiling faces. I'm sorry, but that's just funny! I have never seen a truck with life-size vegetables smiling at me. God is really funny! His signs to us don't always have to be serious. He loves to make us laugh. After all, where do you think our sense of humor comes from?

So, the more J.T. learned to watch and listen for God's signs, the more he would see them. He and I were often in the car for work, so God would often speak to us through bumper stickers, license plates, songs on the radio, signs on the side of the road, sports teams, and a variety of other ways. It was always at the exact moment we would be having a conversation about the possibility of moving that a sign of some kind would appear, and JT. would always notice it. There is no way it was all by coincidence. It began happening more and more. Every time we would revisit the conversation about moving to California, there it would be: a California license plate, an LA Dodgers sticker, or the song "California Dreaming" by The Mamas and the Papas would come on the radio. This went on for several years prior to moving. It got to the point where we would just laugh about it because God would sometimes bombard us over and over again with the signs. So by the time we got to the actual move, we knew beyond a shadow of a doubt that God was leading us out west!

The other circumstance that sealed the deal for us was the fact that my son Matthew felt very strongly that it was time for him to go away to film school in Los Angeles. God worked out all of the details and moved him out to L.A. on very short notice. This left my other two sons and I still living in Illinois, while my daughter was in Minnesota settling into her junior year at college. Within a few months of Matthew being in L.A., we quickly realized that we no longer wanted to stay in Illinois. Circumstances had changed in J.T.'s life, and he no longer felt called to stay in Illinois. It just didn't feel right anymore, especially with Matthew out of the house. There was also the fact that my daughter wasn't planning on returning to Illinois, as she was going to stay in Minnesota after she finished college. With everything changing, we sensed it was finally time to go.

I had no plan. How in the world was this all going to work? Where would we live? Would my self-employed job bring in enough work out there? There was also the fact of how expensive it is to live in California. It's one thing to talk about doing something, but once you actually start doing it, it's a whole new ball game. I had so many questions for God as to how this was all going to look. Funny thing is, God wasn't answering. I knew clearly that He was leading us to move to California, but all I could sense Him telling me was to get the house ready to sell. That's it. Now, I've sold several houses in my lifetime and knew that part wouldn't be too hard, but I was more interested in what would come after that; how it was all going to happen.

Silence. That's what I would get from God, along with confirmations in my spirit that I was just supposed to focus on getting the house ready to sell. This was a bit of a challenge for me, as I felt foolish telling everyone that I was moving across the country without a real plan. Once again, God was asking me to trust Him above what my circumstances looked like. Just like in Genesis, when God asked Abram to leave the land he knew and go to a place that he did not know, Abram had to learn to trust God one step at a time. God did not give Abram the whole picture of how things were going to look, but rather just giving him one task at a time, trusting God had a plan and it would be good. It takes great faith to be this obedient. However, just like with Abram, great faith brings great blessings.

So here I was, back in a place of complete dependence on God. I had to choose whether or not I was willing to trust that He had a good plan for us. The stakes were high, and there was definitely a big risk factor involved with selling most of our things and moving to a place without knowing where we would live. However, after everything we had endured up until that point, somehow it didn't seem so bad. It was a risk we were willing to take. We've always been a very close family, and especially even more so after all we had faced. We knew that if we stuck together and trusted God, it was worth the risk.

Over the next six months, I got the house in order and ready to sell. We had huge garage sales, selling so many things that no longer seemed to have the value they once held. It was so freeing to let so much go. It was refreshing in a weird way. We even sold a car at one of our garage sales! Who knew that could happen? So as we were releasing material things from our life, we were also releasing emotional baggage that was not needed for the next season. It felt as though God was cleansing us in a way, removing things that would ultimately hinder us as we started our new adventure. By letting go of the old things that were occupying our space, we were making room for all the new amazing things God had ahead for us.

"Ok God, so now that I have the house ready, now what?" He then gave me the go-ahead to sell the house. I had known all along that I would sell it by owner in order to make as much money as possible, knowing that we would need every penny for California. I had sold houses by owner in the past, so this part didn't really seem that difficult. It also helped that the house next door to us was up for sale at the same time and brought extra exposure. Within a short amount of time, our house was sold, and for a much higher price than I ever expected. I knew that this was a gift from God, as I was in deep need of a new car, and the extra money from the sale of the house was exactly what I needed to buy one.

I later found out that my house sold for twenty thousand more than the house next to us. The house next door was larger and had more amenities.

If I had known that their house sold for so much less than mine (because theirs sold first), I might have been tempted to lower my price, thinking I was priced too high in comparison to their house. Every time I attempted to find out what price they sold their house for (while I was trying to sell mine), I wasn't able to get the information. God didn't want me to know what the house next door sold for because He wanted me to get more and He knew I would be tempted to think it was listed too high. So, He purposely prevented me from getting that information until after I sold the house. This was just another example of how intentional God is when you are willing to walk in full faith. It was a powerful way for Him to speak to me, as I had struggled with the fact that He was now my only true provider. I had been working on this area with Him throughout my journey of healing, and I felt like this was a sweet kiss from my ABBA Father. Whenever I drive my car now, I am always reminded that it was a gift from Him, and I am still very grateful.

Chapter 14

Walking Off My Map

I kept thinking at this point that surely God would reveal the rest of the plan. The house was sold, all the excess stuff was sold, and things were getting packed as we waited for closing day on the house. *"So, God, where are we going to live?"* I mean, I knew we were going to Southern California, and I suspected that we would want to live somewhat close to Matthew, as he was living in Pasadena, but other than that I was still waiting to get the download of the plan. Oh, but that was not God's plan. He was way more interested in growing my faith even more. There was a point in my life where I was way too afraid to step out in faith of that magnitude and wouldn't move until I knew the next step. As a result, I would usually get stuck in one place for too long. However, God knew that I had now matured enough to go to the next level of trusting Him. So, I had no choice but to wait on Him, as I was now deep in this process and unable to turn back. I chose to trust Him, knowing that He would reveal the next step when He was ready.

Similar to Abraham, I basically just walked off my map. There really is no other way to describe it. I looked up an Extended Stay Hotel in the area somewhat near Matthew and made a reservation, realizing that we had to sleep somewhere when we arrived in California. Matthew's place was just a studio apartment and there was no way we were staying with him, especially with a dog and a bird. Luke decided he would fly out and stay at Matthew's, as there would not be enough room in the car for all of us. Then J.T. and I loaded our precious twelve-year-old beagle and our twenty-two-year-old dove in the car with our luggage and off we went.

We had packed our beds and belongings in U-Haul crates, which were being shipped out to California to be put in storage until we knew where we would live. I can remember driving down the street saying goodbye to the life I had known. Thinking it would be emotional to leave home for good, there was, surprisingly, an incredible sense of peace in the car. J.T. and I both felt amazingly calm. Our dog went fast asleep and our bird was covered nicely in his cage. We did the drive over four days, stopping three nights in dog-friendly hotels along the way. It was a supernatural experience. I don't know any other way to describe it. It was the most peaceful trip. I had never driven across the country before and I truly enjoyed the journey. Other than the craziness of moving a dog and a bird from the car to the hotels three nights in a row, and watching our dog jump from bed to bed trying to figure out where he was, the trip went flawlessly. I could feel God's peace in the entire drive. It was His anointing that we were on the right path.

I can't really describe the feeling I had driving into Southern California for the first time. I had flown into another part of California a few years prior but had never driven into the state from across the country. After living in Illinois all of my life, this was amazing to me. All of the sunshine, the mountains, the warm weather, oh and did I mention sunshine? Sunshine is one of my love languages (if that's a thing). It hit me: this was my new home! OMG! I now lived in Southern California, something I never thought I would say. Although I loved the way I felt as we drove through the mountains and all of the sunshine, I became keenly aware of what was happening on a spiritual level. I could sense God saying to me **"Here you go, I am giving you a completely new start. No more looking back at all of the pain, no more reminders every day of what you lost. Just a lot of sunshine, beautiful mountains, peaceful oceans, palm trees, and new adventures with Me for the rest of your life"**. Breathless. That is the only way I can explain what I was experiencing. God was taking my breath away, turning the arduous journey itself into a beautiful gift.

As soon as we arrived, we settled into the Extended Stay Hotel. God quickly instructed me to start looking for rentals in the immediate area. This proved to be quite the task due to the high demand for rental properties in LA

County. As soon as a property hit the listings, if you weren't one of the first people to respond, you most likely weren't going to get that rental.

The first home we looked at was perfect, but the list of people in front of us was long. It was such a bummer because it had a pool, close to a Trader Joe's (which we love), and in a good neighborhood that seemed pretty quiet. However, we knew it was a long shot. I felt God assuring me to just keep looking. So every day for three weeks, we would go look at as many rentals as we could find, but we never felt like we could make any of them work or stay within our budget. I was starting to realize that this process was much harder than I had anticipated and was really stretching my faith.

Then, out of the blue, I got a text from the owner of the very first house we looked at. The text read: "You are on the top of my list." What? I was blown away, thinking *"How in the world did I get to the top of his list?"* So, I asked the homeowner, "How did I get to the top of your list? There were so many in front of me?" He replied, "Because you are handy, and I want someone to live in the house that can handle small repairs, so they don't have to call me for every little thing." Wow, just wow! I was so amazed! Then I remembered that he and I had talked about several things when I was looking at the house three weeks prior. In one of our conversations, the topic had come up that I was pretty handy at fixing things due to the fact that I had grown up with a dad who was a builder. I had no idea that being handy was important to the homeowner at the time of our conversation, but God did! Isn't God amazing?

He made sure that we talked about that topic, as it would be the catalyst to get us in that house.

We were in awe of what God did. We had found nothing else in the three weeks we spent looking. It felt amazing that the search was over, and we could finally call this place home, for a season. The even funnier part of this story is that because of the way I am wired up, I love to see all of my options before making a decision. Whenever I go shopping for something, I need to see all of my options before I can feel good about choosing what to buy. Otherwise, I feel like I might have missed a better deal. So, God allowed me the journey of house hunting, letting me see all of my options first, before revealing that we did get the house we really liked. God is so good! Now with a place to call home, it was finally time to settle into our new land.

As I settled into our new home, God began to remind me of how a few years ago, I first became aware that I might share my story at some point. I had always imagined that it wouldn't be until I had arrived at some grandiose place in life. Maybe some great career, or amazing ministry. Honestly, those thoughts kept me from writing this book for a long time. I kept thinking, *"Well, when I arrive at some great place in my life, then I'll write the book. Then it will make sense to people. I'll be able to say that I have been through this horrible trauma, but look what I'm doing now."* That's how it seemed to me, like how most comeback stories play out. Then it hit me, or should I say, God, revealed it to me: That's the whole point. I am not living to impress the world as I once was. I am living to please an audience of One. I am living every day to please and honor God, making a difference in the Kingdom of Heaven on Earth, and trusting Him for everything I need. What He thinks is all that matters. While I have known this for most of my Christian walk, for some reason, I lost sight of this whenever I thought about writing this book.

Now let me say, I absolutely love living here in California and know that this is exactly where God wants me, but full disclosure: I have not arrived at an amazing place in terms of the world's eyes. I am living day by day, trusting God for everything. As I said earlier, it is expensive to live out here (not to anyone's surprise), which is challenging for me. It does, however, keep me very close to God, as I know He is my true provider. I also know He did not bring me this far in my journey just to watch me fail. He is in every step of my journey.

The difference now is that I am actually enjoying the journey. After all the pain and grief I've shared with you in this book, I am really enjoying life for the first time in a long time. I'm just a drive away from the beach. There are palm trees everywhere. I get to drive through beautiful mountains every time I leave my house. The sun is almost always shining, and when it rains, it is truly refreshing. Everything is new and I get to explore endless places and meet so many new people.

The very best thing however, is waking up each day knowing that God wants to show me more of who He is, giving me a greater understanding of how much He loves and adores me. You see, in order to truly help others heal from their pain and trauma, I first needed to know who I truly am. There is no better place to run than into the arms of my Heavenly Father. I've discovered that the more I run to Him, the more He shows that He has so much better for me than I ever could have expected, giving me beauty for my ashes.

Recently, God has been preparing me for the next season. He has been teaching me to hear Him and trust Him at even a deeper level than before. He is preparing me for a healing ministry of hope. Although I don't know exactly what that looks like yet, I am certain that I am about to walk into my Kingdom purpose. Things that were spoken over my life years ago are about to become a reality. Although I have not arrived, I am definitely on the journey, and without the journey, we can never arrive at our destination.

So, in the world's eyes, I might still just look like a poor widow, but in God's eyes:

I am clothed in Righteousness!

I am a joint-heir with Christ!

I am a citizen of Heaven!

I am His precious daughter!

And most of all, I am a much-loved child of God!

I think back to that young girl playing with Barbies in the basement, dreaming of her Knight in shining armor. She had no idea of all the pain and joy ahead for her in life. She could never have guessed how broken her heart would become or how beautifully it would be brought back to life. She also didn't realize that while she was dreaming of her Knight on Earth, there was also a Knight in Heaven caring for her. It wouldn't be until she grew up and faced the painful journey that she would realize the truth: *God, the King of all kings, has been and will always be, my Knight in Shining Armor, forever surrounding me, as my protector and champion.*

References

[100huntley]. (2008, December 08). What Happens After You Die? NT Wright on 100 Huntley Street (HD) [Video file]. Retrieved from https://www.youtube.com/watch?v=AQC--9XXpaw&t=23s

[Bethel.TV]. (2018, October 04). Open Heavens | Eric Johnson, Bill Johnson, Shawn Bolz [Video file]. Retrieved from https://www.bethel.tv/events/open-heavens-2018/day-2/7378

Johnson, B. (2018). God is Good: He's Better Than You Think. Shippensburg, PA: Destiny Image* Publishers, INC.

Kendall, R.T. (2012). Why you have to forgive God. Premier Christianity, August(2012).Retrieved from https://www.premierchristianity.com/Past-Issues/2012/August-2012/Why-you-have-to-forgive-God

MacDonald, J. (2010). When Life is Hard. Chicago, IL: Moody Publishers.